A Real Hip Woman

To: Sophia

Thank you for all you do for Women in leadership! you are a Blessing to us ALL!

Jacline Lown-Peters

A Real Hip Woman

Jacline Lown-Peters

XULON PRESS

Xulon Press
2301 Lucien Way #415
Maitland, FL 32751
407.339.4217
www.xulonpress.com

Paperback ISBN-13: 978-1-6628-1923-0
eBook ISBN-13: 978-1-6628-1924-7

Acknowledgements

I would like to thank God for all the blessings and miracles that were given to me! Knowing there was a purpose for my life and knowing you were with me every step of the way gave me Hope.

I would like to thank my parents & siblings who were with me every step of the way. The experience we all shared but never discussed would create in essence trauma for us all. I am sorry for all you had to endure through your life's. For what every reason it was what it was. I love you all!

Thank you to my husband Michael Lown-Peters who for over 40 years has been an amazing husband and partner who took excellent care of me though all of our life challenges. Not many men would do as much as you did to help me get through all my health issues. I Love you!

Thank you to my children Skyler Lown-Peters and Nathan Lown-Peters you both are my proudest accomplishments.

I Love you both!

A special thank you to my very best friend Cynthia Palmer for her love and support and giving me the title of this book.

And last but not least, thank you to all of my friends who are too many to list, you all helped me through all of my life experiences up to this point. Thank you!

Table of Contents

Preface

I have had this book floating around in my mind for over thirty years. I always felt there was a reason for all the pain my family has gone through over the last sixty years. To tell you the truth, I believe the reason was to share some of the amazing things my family and I have gone through. At the age of four, I was injured by a Volkswagen Beetle that hit me broadside. I will cover this in-depth in the following chapters. Scriptures helped me through my struggles, and my message is one of hope and trusting God through the midst of life's trials. Without Him, I would not be here, and hopefully, you will see that we can lean on God through every hardship. By doing so, we can find hope and heal.

My journey is one I hope many do not have to experience. I believe I was spared for many miraculous things to come later in life. I hope this book is an inspiration for you, that you enjoy reading and following what God's plan for my life has been and for you to find your plan.

The Beginning of My Family

My dad, John Jr., was born to John Gordon Lown, Sr. and Elizabeth Lown, née Warner, on November 15, 1931. He was the oldest child. His sister, Joanne, was born six years after him, and his younger brother, James, was born twelve years after him.

My family lived in Binghamton, New York. They were atheists, never went to church, and lived on the family's dairy farm. While growing up in New York, my dad was very active in the Boy Scouts of America and became an Eagle Scout. He learned about American Indian lore, worked with leather, and beaded American Indian clothing. He also gained experience as a leader.

My family moved to Tucson, Arizona, in 1947 when John Jr. was sixteen years old. They wanted to escape the frigid winters. John Sr. said that he had had enough of the winter—it even freezes the cows' ears off. When John Sr. accepted a job offer in Hayden, Arizona, John Jr. had already started at Tucson High Magnet School and wanted to finish his degree. He stayed with a family friend to complete his studies. My dad was also an amateur artist and won many awards for his drawings while in art classes at Tucson High.

Granddad worked in the Asarco Hayden Complex Mines, which now is closed. He was by trade a carpenter but worked for over thirty years at the mine. Grandma was a stay-at-home mom and raised their two small children. She never learned to drive, so Granddad drove her everywhere. In their later years, they would drive to Tucson to shop at their favorite store, Montgomery Wards.

Dad graduated from Tucson High Magnet School in 1949. After graduation, he moved to Hayden and started working for the mining industry on the train rails. He was not happy with the work and decided to join the United States Army in 1950. Grandma was not happy with that decision, nor was his little brother, Jimmy, who admired his big brother.

After boot camp, he graduated and served as a military police officer for ten years. From 1950 to 1953, he was stationed at Fort Holabird within the city limits of Baltimore, Maryland. At the time, it was home to USAINTS, the US Army Intelligence Center and School. His job was driving the car for the four-star general of the base. He was personally chosen by the general because he was not "a drinking man" nor did he use foul language. My dad had the morals of someone the general could depend on to get safely to their destination.

My mom, Verlen Edna Abbott, was born to Vestal Elwood Abbott III and Edna Abbott, née King, in Baltimore, Maryland, on February 10, 1934. She was their second child and eleven months younger than her brother, Vestal Elwood Abbott IV. Verlen was named after her two uncles: Vernon and Leonard. Being named after two men is not something a woman would generally like, and my mom was no exception. I think my grandfather created her name because he wanted his children to share his initials. Later in life, she asked to be called Lynn instead of Verlen.

Baltimore was home to all my mom's family. Her grandparents lived right across the street, and her family lived in a home owned by my great-grandparents. Mom's uncles lived within walking distance all during her youth. They all attended the same Baptist church up the street and walked there every Sunday. They were a faithful Christian family, but only on Sundays.

My mom drew on her faith many times during her life to get through difficult life struggles. Her family was not very wealthy, and they lived simply. My mom grew up with two pairs of shoes, one for church and one for school. My grandfather, Papa, was a firefighter on a fireboat and saved many ships from sinking. He was six-foot-six—a great burly man, loved by all. Nana was five-foot-four and stayed at home. Nana never learned to drive and worked hard at cooking and cleaning to have a nice home.

My mom took after the Abbott genes and was six feet tall in the sixth grade, towering over everyone. She never felt accepted by her father because of how strict and mean he was to her. She felt unloved because she was not the feminine little girl he wanted. When she was eight years old, she slept so deeply that she would wet the bed, and he would make my Nana hang her wet sheets out of the upper floor window for the world to see. I can only imagine the shame she must have felt.

She was told often by her dad, "No man would ever love you or choose you to get married, so you better learn a trade to support yourself."

By necessity, she taught herself to sew and made herself clothes so she didn't have to wear "old lady" clothing, the only clothes made in her size. She wasn't overweight, she was proportionally suitable for her height. Her talents were sewing and clothing design. The things she struggled with then and now were spelling and math. She was able to attend a trade high school. Learning the advanced techniques of sewing, she finished as the top seamstress in the class of 1950. One of her first sewing jobs was in a high-end department store fixing undergarments that were worn back then, such as long underwire bras and girdles. She had learned a trade and become self-sufficient.

When they were fresh out of high school, my mother and her girlfriends would get on a bus and go meet the young servicemen stationed at Fort Holabird. My parents met at the United Service Organization dances every Friday night. There was no alcohol, so most attendees were underage. Their purpose was to dance and have some fun. My mom and dad enjoyed dancing together, and after about a year of weekly dances, they began to date.

My mom, being a strong Christian and wanting only to marry a Christian man, asked my dad to go to church with her, which he eagerly accepted. He soon became a Christian, and asked Jesus into his heart. It wasn't long before they fell in love, got engaged, and were married. My parents, Johnny (as my mom called him) and Verlen, were married in 1953. Mom was eighteen years old and my dad turned twenty years old on the sixteenth of November, one day after their wedding.

Before their wedding, my dad was planning to get out of the Army. He decided to take advantage of the three-month grace period the military provides for someone to re-enlist without losing the time they'd already invested.

They took their honeymoon trip to Hayden, Arizona, where my dad's family lived. My mother, coming from a large city, hated the small-town life. She felt that everyone knew about everyone's business. Plus, she felt like her new family didn't liked her much due to her Christian beliefs.

My dad was able to get hired at the mine working on the train tracks, which were getting updated and replaced. Having grown up in New York and only barely coming out of high school, this was hard labor and not very enjoyable work. He worked side by side with Mexican men, and they wouldn't speak English to him, which he hated. They also felt he was favored over them, which added strife to a difficult work situation. He did not enjoy being a civilian; he liked the rigid lifestyle of being in the Army. So, they were in Arizona for only a little under three months.

When my dad re-enlisted in the Army, he was stationed in Texas at Fort Hood. My oldest brother, Johnnie Dean Lown, was born in Texas in 1954, barely one year from the day our parents were married. When it came to naming him, my father never liked being a junior, so they chose Johnnie and added "ie" at the end to be different from my dad's spelling and to avoid making him "John III." He became a true leader of the family when my dad was gone on his tour of duties. My mom relied on his help with the children.

After Texas, my dad, mom, and brother moved to Fort Wainwright, a military base in Fairbanks, Alaska. This is where my wild-spirited brother Jesse Dale Lown was born barely one year after Johnnie, in 1955.

My mother has stories about living in such a cold and snowy place. Having two babies in diapers, she hung the wet diapers outside to drip dry, and then brought them inside to melt. Once melted, they became soft and pliable. Caring for two children under the age of two was a bit crazy, and remember... this was before disposable diapers were invented!

My family's stay in Alaska lasted for about a year, and then they moved to the Fort Lewis army base in Tacoma, Washington. When my mom found out she was pregnant, she prayed to have a girl who wouldn't be tall like her. (Her prayer was heard. I never grew taller than five-foot-nine and am the shortest in the family).

I am the third Lown child and was born in 1957. Now, if you're keeping count, you'll know my parents had three children under the age of three who were all in diapers. My mom was only twenty-three years old when I was born. I was a bright, beautiful girl, full of life. I had blonde hair, and was the only child with blue eyes like my father.

My name has a bit of an unusual spelling. The story goes that my name had been picked out to be Jean, but when my father saw me after I was born, he put "Jacline" on the birth certificate without the "que" because he said we weren't French. Also, he had a brother-in-law named Gene who he didn't care for. My middle name is Dawn because I was born at dawn. Makes sense to me, but when my mom first saw my birth certificate, it wasn't what she thought it was supposed to be. Fortunately, it was too late to change it because here I am with the unique spelling. I've always liked having a unique spelling. Plus, I prefer Jacline to Jean.

My older brother, Jesse, and I are only one year and ten months apart. We have always been close; we went through most of school in the same classes due to him having an undiagnosed dyslexia disorder. He struggled so much until it was diagnosed many years later after he graduated from high school.

Dad's next assignment was in Berlin, Germany. It was 1958, and he was assigned to be a guard for the Berlin Wall. Mom had the choice of staying in the States or going to be with her husband in Germany. As she'd never felt wanted by her father and had been told she couldn't return home if her marriage failed, she chose to go and be with her husband. They had only been married for four years, and she wanted everyone to be together.

In retrospect, I think she didn't realize how hard it would be to live in a foreign country, especially with three small children. Dad went first, and she was to follow once he had a place for them to live. The plane ride was long and difficult. I can't imagine flying with three toddlers in cloth diapers and who needed food and nursing. It must have been rough.

My parents' fourth child they had was nicknamed a little German girl due to being born in Germany, Joyce Dee Lown, or Joycee to many. Joyce was born on August 9, 1961, days before the building of the Berlin wall, which was constructed overnight on August 13, 1961. Because she was born in Germany, Joyce had to apply for US citizenship once we came back to the States, although I'm sure this made her feel special.

I have often wondered if having a name with a distinct meaning, like Joy, can affect someone during their adolescence, causing them to emulate their namesake. Joyce has more than fulfilled her role as a joyful person. She is gregarious, full of joy, and a friend to all.

East Germany was a communist country, and the East Germans were fleeing to West Germany not to live under the government's control. To stop East Germans from moving to West Germany, the wall was built. My dad was a military policeman for ten years, and during this time in Germany, he was in charge of the troop guarding it. Before the building of the wall, dad said it was a fearful time whenever they saw Russian tanks charging toward the gates. His men had to stand their ground while being intimidated by the Russians. (Historical fact: The Berlin Wall came down on November 9, 1989, ending nearly thirty years of division in the capital city of Germany.)

If you noticed, all the children were named using the same initials: JDL. We only recently found out why—my dad, being an expert in leather tooling, which he learned while being a Boy Scout, had made a leather belt with the initials "JDL" for Johnnie, his first born, and wanted to have all his children be able to wear it as they grew. I wish I knew where it was for the grandkids to use it.

There is one more sibling, Jodi Diane, who was born in 1966. I will tell you her story in the section of living in Tucson.

John
Nov 15. 1953

The Accident, 1962

I have no memory of "The Accident," as it was called by my family. I don't remember what happened or the kind of care I received after it, so the following is what was told to me many years after our family's life-altering event.

It was April 1962, and I was four years old. I adored my two older brothers, Johnnie, who was seven at the time, and Jesse, who was six. My father was still stationed in Berlin, Germany. We lived in a small apartment on the second floor of family housing on the American base.

It was a cold day in April, and my oldest brother, Johnnie, had gone up the street to a park to play baseball. It was dinner time, and my mother asked Jesse to go to the park and fetch him. I asked if I could go along. My mom and dad looked at each other and said, "Yes, that would be okay."

At the park, we called Johnnie and told him it was time to come home.

He answered with, "I'll come in a little while. I'm almost done with the game."

With that, Jesse and I turned back to head home. We came to the major cross street and waited somewhere between the crosswalk and the corner. Jesse and I started to run across the street, but I stopped, ripping my hand from his. I saw cars coming and was scared. As I stood there, frozen with fear, Jesse ran to the other side of the street. I looked to Jesse, and he waited until it was clear and motioned for me to cross. I hesitated and then ran. At that exact moment, a small Volkswagen Beetle came flying around the corner without stopping. It hit me.

The impact was on my left side and catapulted me into the air. I landed on top of the car and then rolled to the ground. It knocked me unconscious and left me lying on the ground. Jesse ran to get our mom and let her know what happened.

My mom said that when she saw me, she heard God say, "I give her back to you!" Once she made it to my side, she laid on top of me and yelled, "Call for an ambulance and don't touch her." She feared that moving me might cause more damage to my body.

An ambulance arrived and took me directly to the emergency room at the Army base hospital. The immediate prognosis was that I had a concussion, and my left leg was broken at the growth plate, just above the knee. Unfortunately, an ear, nose, and throat specialist was on call, not an orthopedic doctor who would have known to check my body completely before body-casting me. The specialist didn't know that children have fragile growth plates. A growth plate fracture at the knee can cause the leg to be shorter, or longer, or crooked if it has permanent damage. But he believed my only problem was a broken left leg.

I was cast quickly to minimize the trauma to my leg and not interfere with the natural length that it would grow. He set my leg and put me in a full-body cast, which started at chest height and went down both legs. Mine had one side that stopped at my right knee and one side that went down my left foot and had an opening at my toes. It also had an opening at the crotch and was cut out around my front and back area for using the toilet. There was a crossbar at my knees to stabilize my legs and could be used as a handle to help move me around. I was in the first cast.

Body Casts

Here are a few memories I have from having to wear four full-body casts that spanned 8 years.

Body Stockings—When any body part needs to be cast, a cotton cloth stocking is put around the body part to protect it from the cast material. It feels like a big sock and is moderately heavyweight. A body cast must be large enough and long enough to fit around the length of the body. Once the casting material is laid on the body, the ends of the stocking are rolled over the edge to protect the skin from the casting material's rough edges. Later I would find out that the stocking material would become a trigger for my post-traumatic stress disorder (PTSD).

Chest to Foot—I was a very late bloomer when it came to puberty. I think it helped not having any chest during my castings. But I was still feminine and wanted to be private. I always wore clothes like a big muumuu dress to cover up my chest and extra-large-sized underwear on my bottom. The last two casts went all the way down my right leg, only leaving my toes out to wiggle, and down my left leg until just past my hip.

Vibrations—Once, when the doctors wanted to check my stitches and progress, the male nurses didn't cut the cast properly. They had to redo the cut opening because they misjudged the location of my scars. I was fearful they would cut me and not the cast. To this day, I can't handle sounds or feelings of vibrations. It throws me right back into the casting rooms; this is another trigger for my PTSD.

Uncomfortable and Inconvenient—This one goes without saying! No showers, no privacy, no bending over, no sitting up, no walking, no swimming, no moving by yourself—you're dependent on everyone for everything. This was a time without remotes, so I couldn't change the television channels. I had younger sisters who were my best helpers. I'm sure they helped with keeping me sane.

Hot, Itchy—Boy, does it get warm, hot, itchy, and stinky. I would use an unbent wire hanger to try to reach the uncomfortable area. I got yelled at a lot for doing this, but at times the itching was unbearable.

No Showers—Water and cast materials don't go well together. I had to have sponge baths, which don't make you feel clean. I never minded the sponge baths, but as I got older, I wanted to take a shower and wash my hair. In the late sixties, a new product came out called PSSSST that was a dry hair shampoo. I was so excited to give it a try. My mother had always washed my hair as best as she could, but it never felt clean. However, all the dry shampoo did was absorb my hair's oils and make my hair feel worse. I hated it. I can remember one time when I was about twelve years old, I was lifted so I could lean over the tub while my hair was washed, and I loved it. There's nothing like that feeling of running water over my head as a child. Oh, the things we take for granted.

Short Hair—I had no choice but to have short hair while I was in my body casts. Because I was bedridden, the back of my hair stayed frizzy and knotted. It was easier to keep it short. When I no longer had to be in casts, I let my hair grow and grow until it was long enough to sit on.

No Privacy—Once the error was at my hip was found, I was turned into a guinea pig. Multiple surgeries were done to try and fix the damage done to my hip. When I was a patient at the Crippled Children's Clinic in Tucson, I was always shown off to interns learning about hip and orthopedic surgeries. By the way, I hated being called *crippled*. What a terrible name for a clinic. Fortunately, the name has been changed to the Children's Clinic in the Square and Compass Building on the Tucson Medical Center campus.

Bedpans—Ugh, my memory of them is awful. If you're in a body cast, you have to use a bedpan to go to the bathroom. I have always had upper-body strength, which helped lift me up to use the bedpan. I would use my buzzer to call the nurses to get the pan in position. After I finished, I would buzz them again, and they would come and take it for cleaning. One time, when I was about twelve or thirteen years old, I was placed in an infant and children's ward in the farthest room away from the nurses' station. They had no room buzzers to ring, so I was given a small, old-fashioned bell made of metal to alert them when I needed help. Each night during the wee hours, I would hit the bell and hit the bell to no response. Then, I would call out. Still no response. I'd had enough of this treatment. I was continually yelled at by the mean military nurses and told I shouldn't wet the bed or that I was trouble and wouldn't follow their rules. When accidents happened, they had to change my sheets. It gave them more work to do. I said, "Put the bedpan next to the bed where I can reach it," because I was capable of getting on it myself. Instead, they kept it in a closet because it was *unsightly* when it was out.

For about four consecutive nights, this happened. I would wet the bed each time because no one came. Do you think a young girl would want to wet the bed? I was pubescent; I didn't want to smell like urine. Then, my cast would get wet and absorb the smell. I was horrified and mad. It was the last straw that broke the camel's back. One night it happened, and I decided I was leaving the hospital. I maneuvered myself to the end of the bed and was balancing on my right cast leg and my free left leg. I was leaving! I got caught hanging on to the end of the bed, but I know if they had not stopped me, I would have left. I told them I was going home to where my mom would take better care of me. It was after this incident that the hospital provided a hospital bed so I could go home and receive proper care. I was *so* happy.

Dad's Broken Back—I usually took ambulance rides to get to my doctor's appointments. But my dad moved me every other time—he'd get me in and out of cars and move me from my bedroom to the living room. Where ever I needed to go, he moved me. I know this was a difficult thing to do. In our home in Fort Huachuca, Arizona, when I was in fifth grade, my mom had made an area in the front living room for me to be able to join the family in the evenings. I had a cot with toys underneath like Barbie dolls to play with if I wanted.

School Intercom System—In 1968, I was in fifth grade and technology was not like it is today. I was unable to attend school because of my body cast. I was getting older and my doctors and school teachers were worried about me falling behind in my studies. It was decided that I would have an intercom system put into my bedroom so I could hear what my classmates were learning. My teacher Mrs. Weiss was wonderful; she visited me daily after school to deliver homework and pick up any papers that were due. She put some thought into it and made the program run smoothly. I would dial the room's phone number, she would answer, and we would put the receivers on the phone to hear each other when we talked. I could also hear my classmates talking.

I began to be known as the girl in the black box. I did this for three months and learned to be sneaky and sometimes cheated on tests. I don't think anyone would have thought I would do that; I was always considered a goody-goody type of girl. I wish I could find my wonderful teacher; I would love to talk with her today and thank her for all the love and kindness she extended to me.

During this time, my dad would carry me down two flights of stairs and put me on a chaise-lounge style lawn chair so I could be outside with the children playing. The change of scenery was somewhat of a relief from being inside. It can be so depressing being unable to move your own body around and depend on everyone for everything.

If you haven't ever had a cast removed, then let me share my experience, which I would repeat two more times in the future. The casting master uses a circular handsaw to cut open both sides of the cast from the armpit to the foot, and then the inside of both legs from front to back. The vibrations were horrific and, as I mentioned, I feared the saw would cut me. It was a horrible experience.

My first encounter with physical therapy came after my first body cast was removed when I was still 4 years old. The therapist told me to walk, but I couldn't. They gave me crutches to use, but still, I couldn't put pressure on my right leg and walk.

After I begged them to stop, I looked at my mother and said, "Mom, I can't walk." The therapist said there was no reason for my immobility. She became angry at my mother. They sent her home and my mother was labeled an overprotective mother. I believe they thought that because my mother stopped me, I just didn't want to walk, which was so far from the truth!

My mother took me home and talked with her German house-maid, Jan. As a child, she had broken a hip and walked with a limp. She was familiar with hip issues, and once both my mother and Jan looked at my hip, they knew why I couldn't walk. My right hip was dislocated! It had been dislocated since the accident three months prior.

Shortly after, it was confirmed that my right hip was dislocated, causing my inability to walk. However, damage had been done to the hip, not only because of the dislocation, but because now my bones were worn away and unable to keep the hip joint in the socket.

The interesting thing is, after realizing that, my hip was indeed dislocated, my mother took me back to the hospital to show the doctor. The first thing out of the doctor's mouth was, "Don't blame me!"

At that time, my mother decided that no one at the army base hospital was going to lay another hand on me. Once my parents decided no one in Berlin was going to provide care for me, they started planning for me to return to the States. My dad received orders to be sent back to the States three weeks later.

My parents, who were very strong Christians and were always active in the church, decided to ask their pastor for help changing his orders to return to the States as soon as possible so I could receive better care for my injury. It had to be God's plan because I was immediately shipped with my mom, two brothers, and my sister to Walter Reed National Military Medical Center in Bethesda, Maryland. My dad stayed to pack up the family's belongings and have them shipped to Baltimore where my grandparents lived. He didn't yet have orders for his next assignment. This happened during the building of the Berlin Wall, and it was a miracle that we were able to move that quickly.

Just recently, I found out that because I was injured in a foreign country, my dad was penalized for the accident because he'd been stationed there. He was reduced by one stripe as a penalty. As if it wasn't bad enough to be dealing with an injured daughter, he had to endure an injured career, too.

A Brave Little Girl, 1963

After leaving Berlin, I was taken to Walter Reed National Military Medical Center in Bethesda, Maryland. The doctors did a thorough exam to see what was wrong. It was determined that my right-hip socket had been worn down so much that the femur bone would not stay in the socket area. The three months of moving around in the full-body cast had done its damage.

The first plan of action was to reduce the hip, which means getting the hip ball properly angled in the socket. It would be my first closed-hip reduction. This was done to repair the dislocation, correct alignment, and restore the joint. After the reduction of my hip was completed, I was put in traction.

Traction straightens broken bones and relieves pressure being put on the bones. It was hoped that the damage of blood flow to the socket would return to a healthy state again—following a period of traction. I was upset because being in traction meant I had to have a six-inch pin pushed through my right leg just above the knee.

One of the very few memories that I have is of this experience is traumatic. I remember receiving merely a local pain killer, so I was alert and watched while they pushed the pin through my right leg. It was a horrifying thing to see. It was a procedure that they should have put me totally under for or at least covered my eyes. I don't think I'll ever forget it: holes in my leg, blood on both sides, and a metal pin going through.

I remember being told, "This won't hurt." Maybe it wasn't physical pain, but it was mentally painful.

The pin provided an anchor with which to attach wires that connected to a pulley system. The system had weights over the end of the bed, which pulled against my leg and configured it into the correct alignment. Being unable to get out of the hospital bed was difficult, and when I moved, it would pull on the metal pin in my leg and was extremely painful. In the beginning, I was in traction with my leg pulled out straight, then they bent my leg up and put a foam square under my leg for support.

During that time, I developed bed sores behind my knees. The nursing staff did not clean me correctly or often enough to prevent perspiration that led to the deterioration of my skin. Neglecting to keep the area behind my knees clean and dry, the nurses allowed me to develop three large bedsores that turned into scars. Two are behind my left leg and one is behind my right. My mom said I was not thriving, and the nurses said I wasn't eating and that I had no interest in life. One nurse took my mother aside and showed her the backs of my knees where my thin skin had started to disintegrate. It wasn't healing and was very painful! I have massive scarring behind both of my knees. I kind of see them as another badge of honor for all the difficult things I've endured.

Once my hip was reduced into the correct position, I became a special situation. It was the beginning of feeling like a guinea pig. No doctor at Walter Reed Hospital had ever dealt with this situation. The team of doctors decided that they would open up my hip, take part of the femur, and rebuild the socket. The socket was so damaged that the hip could not be functional. This was the first surgery I endured.

Once the surgery was completed, which was done through my posterior side, I had another surgery that went through my anterior side. Bone surgery is very painful; I'm sure that is why my memory was kept in the deepest part of my brain. They say our brains never forget, and I believe I have subconsciously suppressed all the memories and pain from that time. My post-traumatic stress disorder (PTSD) will attest to that.

During counseling I had many years later, I realized it is a blessing to have no memory of that time. I don't have memories—just scars to show what I have been through.

I think this is the time I learned to separate my body from my mind. It was a survival skill that served me well as a child, but as an adult, my disassociation made it so I don't realize that I've been hurt or injured for a long time.

During the time I was in the hospital, there was a program for recovering injured soldiers to help care for injured children also in the hospital. I was cared for by one of the corpsmen. I don't remember this man, but in pictures I have from that period of time, he looked like a very caring individual in his twenties.

My mother told me that we got along great except when my bossy side came out, and I kept him running around doing things for me. I never had many visitors while I was in Maryland. My grandparents and uncle lived in Baltimore, so I was fortunate to be able to see them some.

While I was in the Walter Reed Hospital recovering, my dad received orders for his next job. He would be stationed at the University of Arizona in Tucson, Arizona, and work as a recruiter for the Reserve Officers' Training Corps (ROTC). I was left alone in the hospital for four months while my family moved.

When I was left alone for long periods of time, I started to rock myself to sleep. I would get to where my feet touched the end of the bed, and I would push off of it, simulating rocking. I still do this when I'm having a hard time falling asleep. I think it was during this time that I became content with isolation and being a loner.

Physical therapy became a regular daily exercise for me. After the physical therapy, I would be put in a hot tub of bubbling water to help relax my muscles. I truly enjoyed that part of the therapy.

After four months of treatment at Walter Reed, I was released to go to be with my family in Tucson, Arizona.

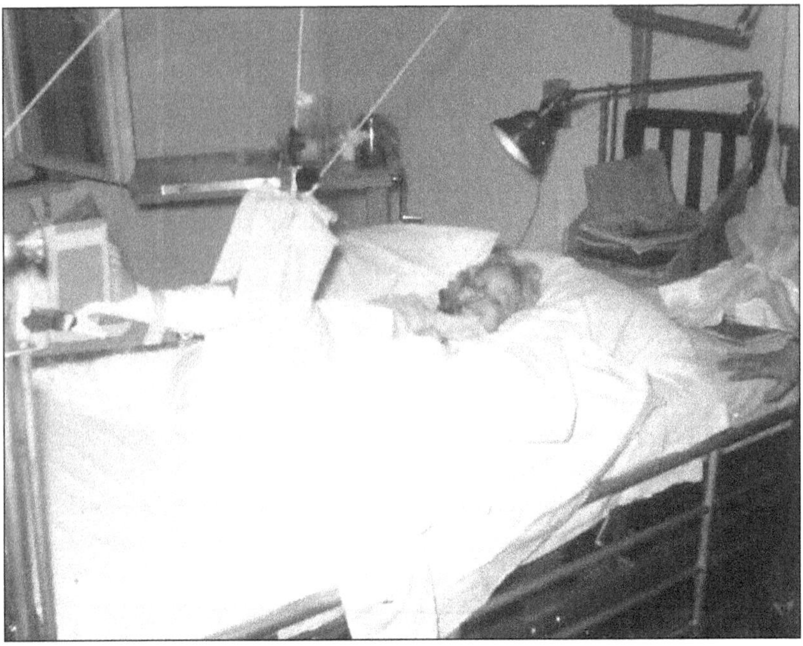

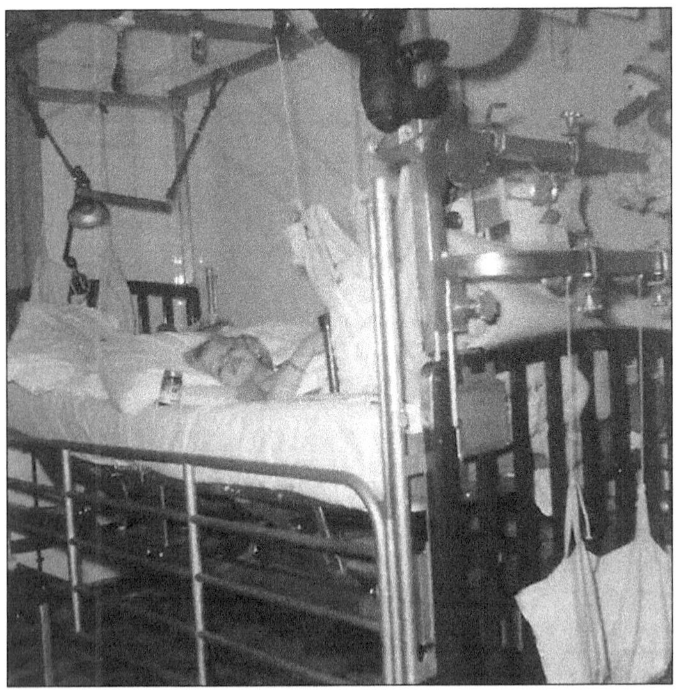

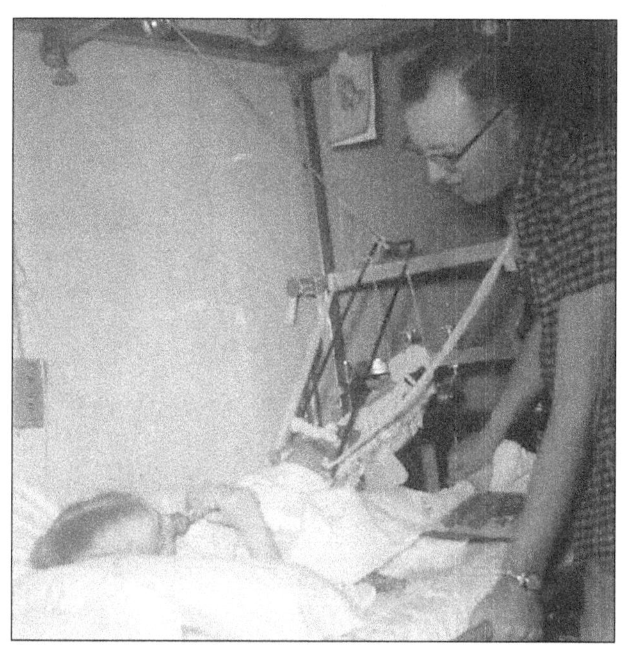

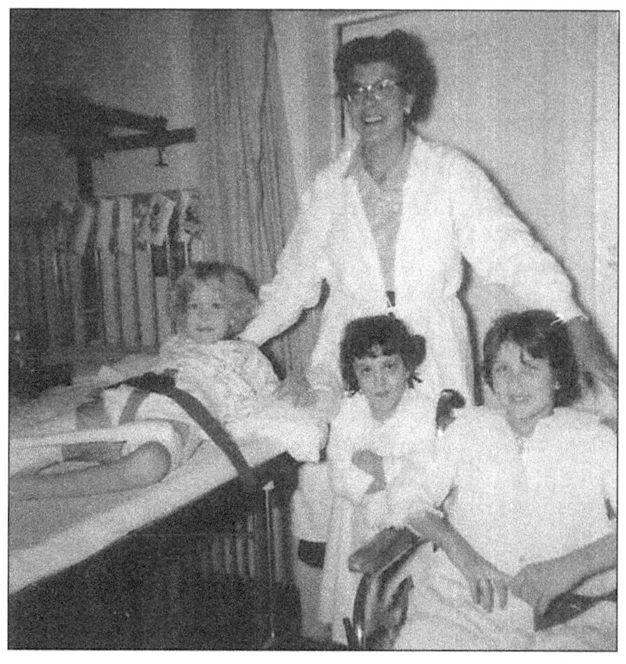

Lost

This is not a story about being lost in the spiritual sense. It is an actual event that I experienced when I was six years old.

In 1963, it was time for me to go to Arizona. From the Army base in Bethesda, Maryland, I was put on a military plane headed to Tucson.

This was all my parents had to go on for three days: (1) I was lost in the military cargo plane system, and (2) no one knew anything about my whereabouts. My parents were beside themselves with worry. One thing that I am sure got my parents through this whole experience was knowing that God knew where I was the whole time.

Nothing is hidden from His sight (Heb. 4:13). He knows our thoughts and our words (1 Chron. 28:9; Ps. 139: 4), and God knows what will happen in the future (Isa. 46:10). God knows everything (1 John 3:20). He knows both you and me intimately (Ps. 139:1-10). He is aware of our broken hearts, each illness, any sorrow we face. He knows!

On the third day, my mother was told that a plane was coming in with a gurney patient on it. My mother was skeptical that it could be me because I could walk, but she went to the airport just in case I was on the plane.

Thankfully, I was on the plane when it arrived and strapped to the gurney. My mother said I was upset that I was strapped to it; I wanted to be walking. She was so glad to see me; she wouldn't let go of me. They had an ambulance there to transport me to our home.

My mother said that she was not going to let me out of her sight then jumped in the back of the ambulance with me.

My mother has filled in the blanks. I have no recollection of this whole experience; I have often wondered exactly where I was. I believe God has protected me through all my experiences, and this was one of the big ones. I know if anything sinister had happened during those three days, I would have told my mother. We were very close; I believe I would have told her.

In my counseling sessions many years later, my counselor said if I had been abused in any way, it would have come up during some of my memory sessions.

I wonder if my experience with being lost is anything like Jonah's.

> *"Now the Lord had prepared a great fish to swallow up Jonah. And Jonah was in the belly of the fish three days and three nights." Jonah 1:17 (KJV)*

His life was changed! Another significant biblical event that happened within three days is Christ's resurrection. Matthew 12:40 references Jonah when it talks about Christ being buried for three days and three nights, which changed all our lives.

I thank God for sending his angels to be with me and protect me. As an adult, I continually remind myself what the Lord said:

> *"I will be with you. I will not leave you nor forsake you...The Lord your God is with you wherever you go." Joshua 1:5, 9*

Once in Tucson, I became a patient at the then-named Crippled Children's Clinic. (Again, what a horrible name! I never wanted to be a crippled child!) Thankfully, it is now called the Shriners Medical Center. Shriners took care of me for several years. The first specialist I saw was Dr. Schwartzman, who I later found out was the first orthopedic doctor in Tucson. I remember him being all business—a gruff man. It seemed like the nurses were afraid of him. He was a brilliant man, and I liked him. He behaved with a very caring attitude.

My first recollection of having corrective braces was when I was five years old. The doctors measured my legs and found there was a two-inch difference in length. The doctors decided to put me in a leg brace. The idea was to take the weight off my right hip while it was healing. Possibly, this would get it to grow and close the difference between each leg.

The metal brace was the length of my leg and had three leather straps that wrapped around my leg. At the knee, two sliding metal pieces would lock in place when my leg was straight. If I wanted to bend my knee, I had to slide the pieces up to allow my leg to bend. Its design relieved pressure from my hip and put no weight on my right leg. But this meant that instead of my foot touching the ground, it was raised three inches up and a metal piece extended from the brace to act as my foot and make contact with the ground. I had to wear corrective shoes that looked like an old lady's shoes. My left shoe was also lifted four inches to make me taller and let my right leg dangle.

I was fortunately not in school yet because it was ugly, especially the shoes. I just wanted to wear sandals or pretty, colored shoes. It was bad enough when I went out to be gawked at, and I know if I had been going to school with the brace on, I would have been bullied by the other kids.

The brace was painful to wear and made sores on my leg. In a few words, I hated it! My mother told me that late at night, once everyone went to sleep, she would find me crawling around the house without it on. I was always trying to break the rules; I hated having to stay put. It was just like when I had to use walkers and crutches. Yuck! I always wanted to be normal, not different, whatever normal is.

After being released from wearing the leg brace, there was only a difference of two-thirds of an inch. I needed to wear a lift in my left shoe or have a lift put on my shoes. My lifts were a cotton-type material shaped in a wedge design. I also had sandals that the shoe repairman glued leather wedges to on the heels. Needing special shoes meant I only had a couple of pairs of shoes. That's probably why I like to have lots of shoes today.

Tucson, 1964

When I was finished wearing the leg brace, I started using crutches. While I was adept at using them, their downside was additional pain. My hands became calloused and my armpits ached. But I liked them better than the walker. After crutches came a cane. I have always hated using a cane, maybe because I feel it is for old people, not someone so young. As I became older, I realized that it is a tool to help me walk farther and become stronger.

My mom always asked lots of questions and was very inquisitive. Once, I remember we had to go down a hall to see another doctor. My mom looked back down the hall and then pulled out the x-ray to look at it on her own. I thought we are going to get in trouble—*stop it, Mom!*

I had to see so many doctors that my mother started a tradition we would do each time before the visit. When I think of tradition, I think of the song in the play *Fiddler on the Roof.* That makes me laugh. But the truth is, there is something about creating a tradition, whether it is for a holiday, a birthday, a celebration, or just to make memories, that can make things a little better.

Before medical appointments, I had to bathe or shower, cut my toenails, and then have lotion smoothed all over me. I have always been very particular in how I want lotion applied to my arms: I want the hair on my arms to lay straight down, not be sticking up. I then made sure I would put on clean, *new* underwear. This was an important one because so many people looked at my hip. When I was young, about seven years old, it wasn't uncommon to have six interns talking to my doctors about the special surgeries that I had gone through. My clothes also had to be easily removable and easy to put back. I could never have metal on my clothes, like zippers or buttons because of my X-rays. When I was older, I always shaved my legs to be smooth.

Before a doctor visit, my mom would take me out and buy the prettiest and most feminine lingerie and peignoir set; it had to be frilly and beautiful. I remember once I had a beautiful white set that looked like a bride would wear on her wedding night. It had a flowing gown and a matching sheer robe. They had to be long and flowy. My other sets usually were pale pink or sea foam blue. (Don't you just love that color's name? It makes me think of being at the beach, which is something I always love.) Somehow this small ritual helped make everything better and doable!

But no matter the ritual or tradition that we followed, somehow I could never sleep before a doctor visit or surgery. As I grow older, I have learned to just roll with it and spend time praying and trusting all will be fine, truly having the peace that passes all understanding.

I was known as a pretty social girl in grade school, excited to be out of braces and mobile. My brother and I were attending Roskruge elementary school in Tucson. I remember in second grade, I was told many times by my school teacher to stay in my seat and keep my mouth shut. I was warned several times, and the last warning was: "If you don't stay in your seat and stay quiet, I will tie you to your seat and tape your mouth shut." I must have not believed her because, during recess, she took a jump rope and tied me to my seat then taped my mouth shut for the whole time. Unbelievable! If that would happen now, the teacher would probably be fired. I know from that time on, I would listen and be still. Never an easy thing for me to do.

Exodus 14:14, The LORD will fight for you; you need only to be still...Psalm 62:5, For God alone, O my soul, wait in silence, for my hope is from him. Psalm 46:10, He says, "Be still, and know that I am God; I will be exalted among the nations, I will be exalted in the earth."

During our time in Tucson, my dad was actually in Korea or away in the summers to teach military tactics. I remember for a short time, we lived in a house on the University of Arizona campus. In our backyard, we had rabbits, mice, and turtles. My sister Joyce would wear an apron and walk around with the mice in her pockets. We loved the animals.

Summers in Tucson were awesome. I remember having a fruit and vegetable truck going down our street, usually on Saturdays, and we would all run out and choose some fruit. My mom would come out and pick out fresh fruit and vegetables to use when cooking. The truck was owned by a man named Tobias. He was an older man, and the truck looked like it was from the 1920s. It was green and very old. He had baskets just filled with freshness all around the bed of the truck. It had an awning to keep the sun off the food. We always looked forward to him coming.

In later years, we would go to the old Jewish Community Center and go swimming. There was Tobias in his swimsuit, enjoying being outside and having fun. He looked different, and when he left, he drove off in a new Cadillac. It is always best not to make a judgment based on what people look like. We always thought he was a poor man, but that was just his working persona.

Our other favorite summer activity was to swim in the pool at the University of Arizona. There was a pool with a gym next to it called Bear Down Gym. All of us older kids were on the swim team, and we were awarded many ribbons for racing and coming in first, second, or third place. We were all great, but my wild brother Jesse was the best and fastest. He did amazing jumps off the diving board. One summer, my brothers decided to get Mohawk haircuts. The haircut lasted only one summer for Johnnie, he hated the Mohawk. I fondly remember those swim meets and all my sunburns.

We spent hours at the pool because we were there most of the week. My friend and I would go exploring in the Bear Down gym. Although we were not allowed, we would venture out to the upper floor. The only problem was that we had to go through the men's dressing room. We had to pass the showers, which was always exciting because sometimes men were showering while we snuck in. We had to go through to the back of the dressing room and go up a heavy wire staircase to get to the upper room. It was huge, a room full of exercise equipment and trampolines. We only stayed up there for a short while and played. Fortunately, we were never caught, and no one was ever up there exercising.

My friend and I did many things together. I did not always act like a good Christian girl. Instead, I was a follower. One time my friend convinced me to go into a neighbor's house by climbing behind a hedge and sliding the window open. It was easy; we got in and looked around, just checking it out. But breaking and entering is not an acceptable way to live. This was someone's home, and we got caught. We were taken to the police station and talked to. We didn't get arrested, but we were scared. We both had to go to counseling and promised never to do it again. My counselor said she wasn't surprised that I did this because of my medical history and lack of a normal childhood. It was an embarrassing thing I did, and I promised I learned my lesson, but later I'll share another peer pressure event in my life. I guess I didn't learn my lesson after all.

Another family hobby we had was Boy Scouts. My brothers both participated, and my parents were leaders. As a boy, my dad had received the Eagle Scout Award, and he wanted to share his love of Boy Scouts with his two sons and three younger girls, so we were able to attend each meeting. We felt like we were also scouts.

When my parents were responsible for putting on summer camps, we would all go up to Mount Lemmon, just north of Tucson.

One time, while my dad was in Korea, my mom and the other leaders of our troupe put together a summer trip to Rocky Point in Mexico. There were four adults, one was my mom, and there were ten Boy Scouts plus me and my sister, Joyce. What an incredible experience we had. On the first day, the old bus that was our sole transportation broke down. Stranded on the side of the street, the adults decided to find a place to get the bus repaired so we could get on with our trip. We were close to the beach, and they unloaded our luggage there so we had a place to sleep.

The sun was setting, and it was beautiful! It looked like the end of the world. I am sure this was when I developed my love for the ocean.

That first night was incredible until about two a.m., when we all woke up to find ourselves sleeping in the water. Everything we had was wet. Whoever had chosen where to put the tents didn't take a high tide into consideration. So, needless to say, we were running around trying to get all our stuff from going out into the sea forever.

We were only there for five days but what a time we had. Out in the distance, we could see some lights on a building. Tomorrow we would investigate. What we found was a bar that was only open in the afternoon until early in the morning. They had crabs and chickens, and they would pour liquor over the animals and have them fight. We had no idea what the men were saying, but you could tell they were betting and wanted them to fight. This was the only thing I didn't like about Rocky Point, but it did give us an experience to remember. It was gruesome, and I wondered how these men thought it was entertainment.

Being in Rocky Point was one of the best summer experiences that I remember during the time I felt like a Boy Scout. Truly a trip I won't forget.

We only lived on the University of Arizona campus for a year, then we moved to a rental house on Fifth Street, practically across the street from the elementary school we would be attending. The owners had put their stuff in a big city bus that was parked in the area behind the house. They also had a wooden chopping block for making firewood. We had a great basement. The temperature never got up beyond sixty-four degrees, and it was directly out our back door and down the stairs under the house.

One year my mom decided to make root beer. That was a fun project. Making all these bottles of root beer and sealing them. They were supposed to ferment for a set amount of time, then they would be ready to enjoy and drink. But before they were ready, we heard the popping and banging of bottles exploding in the basement. The whole batch was ruined; what a mess we had to clean up. The walls of the basement were rocks that had been taken out of a volcanic mountain, so they were very porous. It was a mess.

The washing machine we used at the time had a tub underneath and a crank handle, that squeezed the water out of the wet clothes. My mom had me help with the laundry, which seemed like a never-ending job between washing and ironing. That might be why I hate ironing. I remember these metal forms we would use to put my dad's pants in. They were the length of the pant leg, and they would separate to stretch out the pant leg until it was taut. It stayed in the pants until they were dry. The material would dry so hard and stiff that the pants could stand up on their own. It was a great way to get out of having to starch and iron them.

When we had ironing days, my mom would put the clothes in a bag while they were still damp, pull them out of the bag, spray them with starch, and then iron them. Our clothes were mostly cotton, and they desperately needed to be ironed or else they were a mass of wrinkles. Before polyester material was created, there were people who even ironed their bedsheets. Crazy! Seems a big waste of time.

After being in a body cast and being bedridden so long, I had to have short hair because the back of my head would become matted. So when I was able to grow out my hair, I wanted it to grow, grow, grow. Unfortunately, with long hair comes with more responsibility. When I was about nine, my mother kept warning me that if I didn't comb my hair and take care of it, she was going to cut it short. I didn't believe her, so I didn't comb or brush my hair because it hurts when you have knots in the back. Once again, I was warned. My mother would usually give us three chances to change our behavior before she would dole out the consequences. And sure enough, she warned me again, and I chose to ignore her. It wasn't too long after that last warning that she cut all my hair off into a pixie cut. I thought my mother was the meanest, hardest person ever! But after tears and me screaming, I settled down. I liked my hair, it was cute and curly and less work. This truly was a case of mother knows best.

My mother is a very creative person. She knew I would remember this experience, so she kept my chopped hair and used it as stuffing in the velvet needlepoint pincushion she made for me. I still have it, but I chose never to use it. Instead, I've treasured it as a gift from her. The cushion is round and the size of a large apple. It has black velvet sides with a picture of a cross in needlepoint on the top. It will always be a remembrance of that haircutting event.

In 1966, my youngest sister, Jodi Diane Lown, was born in Tucson. Being only nine years older than Jodi, we are very close. My dad was stationed in Korea shortly after the time of her birth. He served as a senior instructor at the Second Infantry Division demilitarized zone patrolling school and was gone most of Jodi's first year. With five kids and no dad, it became the responsibility of all the older children to assist with taking care of the younger children.

To help my mom, we would serve her breakfast in bed. We would cook pancakes and bacon, and then put a flower on the food tray with a cup of hot coffee. One morning, we were all excited about delivering breakfast. We took it into my mom's room and whoever was carrying the tray ran into Joyce, and the hot coffee ran down her tiny arm. We all screamed! It was horrific, one of the worst times I remember growing up. My mom flew out of bed, and I think she put gauze on it before we jumped in the car. She drove like crazy to the Davis-Monthan Air Force Base. Joyce had third-degree burns down her arm and wore a huge bandage for quite a while. It is a miracle her arms weren't scarred.

We also had a scare that my brother Jesse would not make it through a dare from one of his schoolmates. It was while attending Roskruge elementary school. Jesse was undiagnosed with dyslexia and struggled through school with reading and was a frustrated child. Since he couldn't excel in academics, he excelled in sports, basketball in particular. One day after school, he got in a fight and was dared to jump over the steps at the front of the school. There were at least eight or nine steps. He did it and was dared to do it again, which he did. The first time went great, but he hit a patch of sand the second time. His feet slid out from under him, and he slammed his head on the last step. He was immediately knocked out. At the time he did this, I was in the restroom and some girls came to get me to tell me what happened. I immediately ran to the front of the school. He was unconscious, and the nurse was there, holding his head. He had a goose egg bump forming on the back of his head.

The ambulance came, and they took him to the hospital at Davis-Monthan Air Force Base. My dad was in the Army, but we went to the base for any medical needs. It was a scary time for the whole family. We didn't know if he would be okay. Thankfully, he woke up, and although it did take time for him to heal, we praised God that he was healed.

Years later, I would hear my mom say how bad she felt when she learned she could have taken both Jesse and Joyce to a closer hospital, but it was done and in the past.

We were an active family. My mom and dad were Boy Scout leaders and had weekly meetings. I was in Girl Scouts and loved all the things that we did. I was awarded most of the badges you could earn. I started as a Girl Scout Brownie and then became a Girl Scout. Having a dad who loved being involved with many people and activities means we never had time to be bored. One of my best memories as a child while living in Tucson was when we had entertainment night. My two sisters and I would dress up in these red shorts with lace on the legs and white T-shirts. We would do skits and sing and just try to entertain anyone who would watch. It was such fun!

Those first years in Tucson made many memories, both good and bad. Since my dad was gone every summer, it always felt like we didn't even have a dad. My mom was very strict and had to make tons of rules to keep order in a house with five children. My older brother Jesse struggled in elementary school with undiagnosed dyslexia and was held back a year because of it. In retrospect, I am sure there were times my mom felt guilty about my accident despite her juggling four other children and having a military husband who was often gone.

Behind the house my parents rented, the owners had a big green bus in the backyard that was full of their stuff. There was a rope hanging from a huge tree that we could swing on. There was also a big log outside and Jesse used to chop up its wood whenever life was confusing and frustrating. It seemed to help him get past the frustration.

I remember once when Jesse kept taking my socks and running around outside with them, I complained to my mom and said, "Jesse won't stop wearing my clothes." She said to Jesse, "If you want to wear her clothes, then just put on a dress."

The next thing we knew, Jesse was wearing one of my dresses, a pair of my socks, and my shoes. He was in the backyard chopping the wooden block like crazy. That was probably the angriest I had ever seen him. It was a difficult life, but we all loved each other, and we got through it the best we could.

When my dad returned from Korea, the family was transferred to Fort Huachuca in Arizona. But after a short stay, he was off again. In 1969, he received orders to go to Vietnam. There, he was first sergeant of the 101st Airborne Division (Air Assault) and received the gold medal, silver medal, multiple excellent conduct commendations, among numerous other metals.

Fort Huachuca, 1968

In 1968, when I was almost eleven years old, I had my second and third body casts. Due to the damage done while in the last body cast for three months, my hip bones were rubbing against themselves and became unstable. The socket would not hold and could have possibly dislocated. I was told to only walk and never run. I had been under the care of the Crippled Children's Clinic in Tucson. I was under the care of them for several years and one of their specialists, Dr. Schwartzman. He designed a surgical method to make my hip more stable. It involved taking part of my femur bone and grafting a ledge onto my worn-down socket to give it more protection. Then, they would cut my femur bone and angle it more inward. This would make the hip bone secure and less easy to displace.

Due to the complexity of the surgery, the doctors used pins to hold the bone grafts in place, which meant two separate surgeries were needed, one to pin the bone grafts in place and one to do everything else. I needed to be in a body cast after each procedure, which happened three months apart.

The doctor assisting Dr. Schwartzman became my favorite doctor of all time—Dr. Hugh Thompson. I was a patient of his for twenty years, and he eventually did my total hip replacement.

Body casts are, thankfully, rarely used now. Over the years, it was discovered that getting up and moving after major surgery is better than being bedridden.

Two years later, I had another surgery to remove the pins and plate. (Their official names were Smith-Petersen Nail and Thornton Plate.) I always had problems when the anesthetist tried to start IVs for each surgery. My veins are deep and like to roll. Once, I had two doctors, one on each side of me, patting my arm to get a vein to rise.

They both kept apologizing, saying, "We don't want to hurt you." I was grateful to have a very high pain threshold. It wasn't hurting me, I just wanted them to find a vein and get started. During this surgery, I woke up. I remember realizing I had forgotten to tell them that I wanted them to save the pins for me. As I told them this, I heard the panic in their voices as they said, "She's awake, she's awake. Give her more morphine." I didn't feel any pain, so all was well. But I never did get the pins like I'd wanted.

Around this time is when I can actually remember my childhood. It is kind of weird to only remember different surgeries because of what I have been told. Somehow, I believed that I was going to be free of the pain I had continually dealt with. I thought that after my last surgery, I would be free, and my conscious memory would wake up and keep track of my enjoyable life. We don't realize how our subconscious mind remembers everything.

It is interesting how our minds work to protect us from the constant pain we may feel as a child, especially when we cannot yet cope with trauma. I, at times, wish I could remember everything, but the pain must have been truly unbearable. Why else would I have no memory of the events?

I learned very early on that I could leave my body and turn within to distance myself from chronic pain. Later in life, I would learn that meditation and distractions such as music can help with the pain.

My memories of living in my body casts are numerous and unpleasant. In writing this book, I have become aware that reliving and documenting my life experiences has its drawbacks. I want to share my experiences because I believe that my faith is what has brought me through many difficult and horrible experiences. Without my faith, I don't believe I would have survived.

These are some of my memories from that time. My mother is a great seamstress, she always made my dad's Civil War reproduction uniforms, and she accepting sewing jobs from the community. I learned to sew because I was taught to do her hand sewing. I hemmed pants and dresses, which gave me something to do, and I became great at it, too.

My mom always seemed to have a horrible time while she waited for my surgeries to end. She was insanely nervous. One time, she wanted to make me something special while she waited for me. She made me a beige and turquoise cat-face pajama bag. When I saw it after the surgery, I said, "Mom, I think the eyes are crooked." She started laughing and said she didn't think I would notice.

After my last surgeries, I wanted to grow out my hair, since I could take care of it myself. I enjoyed it growing. My great-grandmother Mattie never cut her hair, and it had grown so long it touched the floor. She only washed it once a year and wore it upon her head in a bun. Eventually, she went bald at the crown of her head because of that hairstyle. When my mother talks about her grandmother, she says she had a distinct smell. I'm sure her hair would stink because she lived in Baltimore where it's hot and humid, and she only cleaned it once a year. But she motivated me to see how long could I grow my hair. Except, unlike my great-grandmother, I would brush and wash it so it would never have a bad smell or odor. The longest I grew my hair was past my hips—I could sit on it.

Being in and out of body casts for over eight months made me pretty much dependent on everyone for everything. I learned very early how to manipulate my siblings as well as the adults around me. I didn't realize at the time that they all were suffering themselves from massive guilt over the accident. In retrospect, I feel terrible that

I did that. I'd became a very spoiled and privileged child because of my ability to manipulate.

While in a body cast, I usually took ambulance rides to my doctor's appointments. My mother put a military cot in the front living room so I could be with the family in the evening. I remember getting carried from room to room.

As for the other times, I was moved in and out of cars or moved from my bedroom to the living room by my dad. I know it was a difficult thing to do. It is so easy to get depressed when you can't leave the house or the hospital. My family was very aware of this. Many times, they would get my dad to move me to the back seat of the car and take me for a car ride. I would fill up the back seat. I'm sure my dad's back suffered due to my size. You see, I have always been a big girl. My heritage is Scandinavian and Viking, i.e., I am tall with large bones. Sometimes, we went to a park for a picnic, and I would sit in the back seat with my casted leg out the opened door to rest it on the dirt. This helped immensely with my cabin fever. Just seeing something different was great.

It was during this time that I used an intercom system to virtually go to school. When I was attending school through the intercom, I didn't know any of my classmates. Because of this, I feel like I missed out on learning to be social and friendly. My counselor said that what I endured in terms of abandonment, isolation, and restrictions could have been permanently disabling, leaving me fearful and relationally stunted and bitter. I am grateful that with God's grace, I became an overcomer.

To the kids at school, I was just a disembodied voice in a black box. My parents thought of a great way for me to meet the students in my class—throw a birthday party. Due to the size of the class, it was decided to only invite the girls over to our house for the party. It was a fun idea, except I think this only perpetuated the idea that I was different. I felt like all the girls came to the party because they were curious about me and wanted to see what I looked like in the body cast. I felt like I was in a freak show. I think after that experience, it was better for me to be alone and not try to join in with groups.

It's always been easy for me to be a loner and be by myself. I think it's because of all the times I couldn't attend things or was in hospitals. My socializing was always kept to a minimum; I never had many friends. My siblings were all I had. But once, while I was in the hospital after one of my surgeries, one of my friends wanted to come to visit me, but the hospital would not allow her to visit my room because she was under eighteen years old and not a family member. They put me in a wheelchair and rolled me to the window. I was on the third floor of the hospital. It was so special to see my good friend Julie waiving at me from down on the ground.

Our large family didn't always go on vacation, but once we went to the Phoenix Zoo and enjoyed seeing the animals face to face. Jesse taunted the elephants, and I told him to stop, but of course, he didn't listen to me. The elephant didn't like it, and he filled up his trunk with water and sprayed both of us. We were dripping wet. All we could do was laugh and know that we would dry fast under the summer sun.

Another great memory I have is going to Disneyland. My youngest sister, Jodi, was too young and didn't go. Instead, she stayed with one of our neighbors. We were so excited about Disneyland. Off we went in our station wagon to California.

The only thing we were not prepared for was the weather. A cold front came in, and it was freezing. My parents said, "Let's go shopping." They found a Salvation Army thrift store. Since my mom was a great seamstress, we rarely went shopping. It was awesome to pick out warm clothes with my sibling, so we wouldn't freeze. We also went to Knott's Berry Farm and Universal Studios and stopped to see the parting of the great seas. Although we didn't vacation often, we never felt deprived or unable to enjoy life. Our parents did a great job raising us.

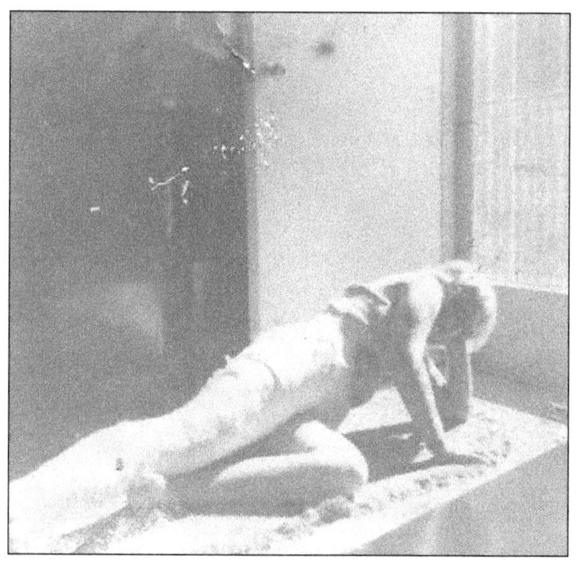

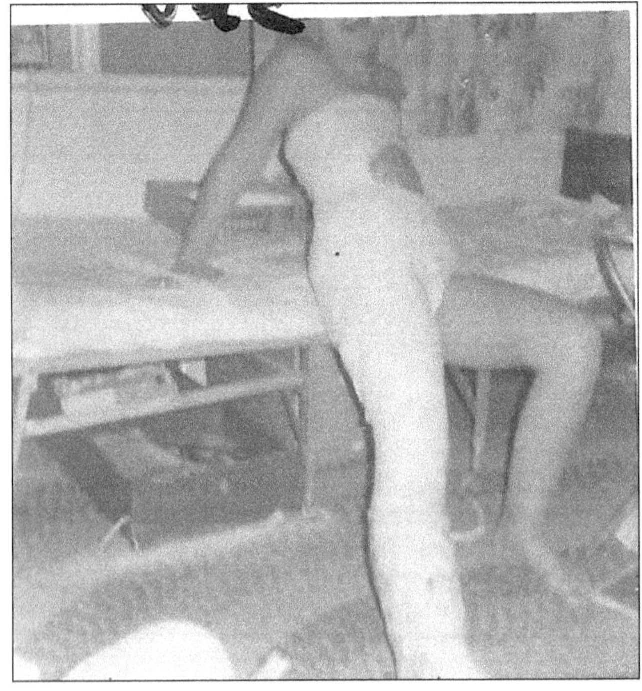

The Seventies

The remainder of my dad's five-year reenlistment was in Fort Huachuca, Arizona. In 1970, my dad retired after twenty years of service in the Army, achieving the highest rank of enlisted men: first sergeant. Before it was decided that he would retire to Tucson, my parents had done some research on other towns. One of the options was Tombstone, Arizona. My parents loved the historical reenactments. Additionally, they had created a mail-order business that sold Civil War reproduction uniforms and paraphernalia that my dad designed and my mom created. It seemed like a great fit, up until they asked their children. The three teenagers unanimously decided that we would hate living in a tiny, rural, historical town. So, Tucson it was.

Even during the difficult times I'd spent in body casts, and during the times my dad was absent, we were able to do many different things. While recovering, I had to use wheelchairs at times to get around. I'm grateful that I didn't have to use them for long periods of time. When I was about thirteen years old, my family went to Old Tucson for the day. Let me tell you, Old Tucson at that time was not set up for handicap access. My brothers took turns pushing me around on either dirt or wood plank walkways. It was a terrible time for all. I ended up sitting under one of the covered areas while everyone else went sightseeing.

The base had many opportunities for activities for military dependents. There were Saturday matinees that would play two movies back-to-back for free. We also attended school dances and after-school activities. My mom had decided that when we need a ride home from an activity, we would call home and let the phone ring three times and then hang up. It wouldn't cost anything, and she would know it was time to go pick us up. We would miss those things when we moved to a much larger town.

On the way home from one of my doctor's appointments, my sister Joyce had a stomachache. We were in the station wagon; my sister and brothers were in the back seat. I was up front with my little sister Jodi asleep between my mom and me. My sister said she didn't feel very well, leaned forward from the back seat, and threw up all over my little sister's head. My mom pulled the car off the highway and tried not to wake Jodi as she cleaned her up. The rest of us were laughing. Just then, a highway policeman stopped to check if everything was okay. When my mom rolled the window down, he immediately moved back from the smell. We all continued to laugh. Jodi doesn't appreciate us telling this story, but I find it hilarious.

There was a time when I would do anything to be a friend to someone. That type of peer pressure is the worst. It was a week before my dad was transferred to Tucson, and I was with a girlfriend in the bathroom at school. I can't even remember who or what she looked like, not even her name. But that day I wanted to be liked and she challenged me to write on the bathroom mirrors. Someone had left lipstick on the sink, and she said, "Let's write something dirty." She started writing and dared me to do the same. I picked up the lipstick and wrote the F-word. At that moment, another girl walked in and saw what we were doing. That was the beginning of the end of my time at that school.

I was called out of my class to go see the principal. He was not very happy with me. He told me what the other student saw when she went to the restroom. I had defaced school property. I would be suspended for three days. But in one week, we were moving to

Tucson, so he said I could attend the next two days and then not come back to finish the week. He also said he was very disappointed in me, that I had always been a good student, and this behavior surprised him.

When the day was done, I had to face my mother. I knew it wouldn't be fun. I was dreading how upset she would be about what I had done. She was furious, and I tried to blame the girl who talked me into it, but it didn't work, I had done something bad. Thankfully, this experience would be behind me once we moved to Tucson.

1971

After we moved to Tucson, my dad started looking for a second career. He worked at Old Tucson for a short time driving the stagecoach and then worked as head of security for printing and transportation at Tucson Medical Center for three years.

My brother Jesse was a wild, athletic, handsome, and a ladies' man. It was 1971, and we were in the eighth grade at a new school. I was an embarrassment to him. I wasn't ugly or overweight at the time but was very insecure and had a little limp. We had just moved from knowing everyone at a small school to a middle school with three times the population. There's nothing like feeling like an outsider.

To add to those issues, my brother started telling people the reason we were in the same grade was because I was adopted. *What*? Boy, that hurt. I loved my brother and couldn't believe he was saying that. It is true that we don't look alike. I take after our dad's side of the family with fair skin, he takes after our mom's side of the family with dark skin. In the summer, Jesse gets very tanned and doesn't burn. I'm the opposite and burn like crazy. In retrospect, he was just trying not to be embarrassed about being held back a grade. My experience with physical education (PE) at that school was just as bad.

The PE class in Fort Huachuca had a very lax dress code, you could wear anything during class. While in Fort Huachuca, my mother the seamstress made me a cute, white sailor outfit. It was adorable, but the PE teacher wanted each student to have their names on their outfits. She took a black marker and wrote my last name in black, and the ink ran! My mother was so mad at the teacher for doing that, it did look bad. She asked why the teacher didn't let her make a patch with my name so it didn't bleed and look bad.

When we relocated to Tucson, the PE class had a dress code, a blue shorts jumpsuit. I was good with that, but my mom wanted me to wear the white outfit, so she wouldn't have to buy one. When you have five children in school, there is a never-ending need to buy things. My mom went to the school to argue her case and won. I could wear the white sailor suit, making me stick out big time! This added to my insecurity. Another outfit my mom made me was a long vest and knickers. It was the seventies, and my mom wanted me to be stylish. Little did I know that she was a future business owner of a costume shop, and I was her guinea pig. I only wore the outfit a couple of times because, like I said, I stuck out like a sore thumb.

When I picked out my middle school classes, my mother insisted I take home economics. Part of the home economics requirement was sewing, I had to make a "skort," which is a pair of shorts with the look of a skirt. When I brought them home, I was so proud of them. But my mother looked at them and said it was all wrong—what were the instructors teaching me? She made me take out the mistakes she saw and redo it under her direction. I didn't want to take the class in the first place, and now I knew why.

My eighth-grade experience in Tucson lasted only five months, which I think had to do with the food addiction that I'd developed. I began eating my feelings because it was impossible to feel like I fit in, and I gained weight. These stories seem so insignificant now, but at the time, what happened to me was a huge deal. I didn't know it then, but I was developing an enmeshment relationship with my mother.

Many years later, I would learn enmeshment means being loyal to the person you are enmeshed with. It was a love-hate relationship in full rage. I still struggle with the unhealthy relationship my mother and I share. I know that my mom did the best she could with all that had happened in her life. Yet, it still saddens me to look back on her strength that at times overwhelmed me to the point of fear. I did not want to compete with her in any way.

During the time of my dad's station at Fort Huachuca, my mom and dad started a mail-order company making reproduction civil war uniforms. Dad had a love for history, especially military uniforms, and had developed a great collection. It wasn't unusual for my siblings and me to be dressed in period costumes, participate in parades, and win many awards for our costumes.

Mom had started working part-time at a costume shop on Saint Mary's Road, but shortly after she started working, the shop closed. That was when mom got the idea that she and dad should open up their own costume store, which became Lown's Costumes, Inc. When they started, my dad went to college on the G.I. Bill to learn business accounting and received an associate degree.

The costume shop became a very successful business and supplied costumes to the Tucson community for thirty-five years until closing in 2007. Dad became a lifetime member of the National Costumers Association in 1997. Early in the life of the business, he would create entries for the Rodeo Parade using popular costumes at the time. One such entry involved four of his children dressing up as the *Planet of the Apes*. It was a scary endeavor trying to learn to ride a horse down the back alleys of South Tucson with a mask on. That might be considered child abuse now, but for me, it was a funny memory.

Moving up to Tucson from Fort Huachuca was a shock to my whole being due to the number of students in each class. In Fort Huachuca, the classes were smaller than in Tucson. I became a fearful young lady, afraid of everyone, and very insecure. I believe all the things I had been through molded me into a very self-centered person. Because I couldn't attend school regularly at the beginning of my life, I missed some of the social graces you learn in middle school.

My first experience with banking happened while attending Doolen Middle School. At the time, Wells Fargo bank would come every Friday to educate those who wanted to learn by having a finance and money management class. They taught us to open a checking and savings account, fill out deposit slips, and write checks. I think it was a great educational tool. I babysat almost every weekend, so I was able to learn how to manage money correctly. Educating young adults on money management is a huge asset that helps them learn practical and important life skills.

436

1972

As if middle school hadn't been scary enough, I was sure attending high school would top anything I had experienced.

I played the flute in the high school marching band. I was walking better and wanted to participate in it. The Tucson Las Vaqueros Rodeo Parade was happening in February, and we practiced up and down the streets around the high school, making sure we were in step while playing music. We got our uniforms and were ready to go. My dad has always been a parade enthusiast, and I had been in many parades and seen so many that I knew what to expect. We got there early to set up, and then off we went. We did great, and I walked all five miles! I think that was the farthest I have ever walked without stopping. I was tired but proud of myself.

Jesse always seemed healthy, but whenever he got hurt, he came close to death. His first brush with death happened when he jumped down the steps of our elementary school. Gratefully, he recovered fine from the jump, but we weren't sure what would happen during his second accident. It was a cold winter in Tucson, and my brother was cold. He went outside to get a sleeping bag out of the shed.

During the night, Jesse was bitten by a black widow spider that was inside the sleeping bag. My brother was in the hospital for a week, and no one was sure when he would come home. Our prayers were eventually answered, and we realized that although Jesse was rarely hurt, his injuries tended to be life-threatening when they did happen.

1973

I loved being a member of my family church, Catalina American Baptist Church in Tucson. While American Baptists are more liberal than Southern Baptists, my church still believes in and teaches the Bible. Many retired pastors came to preach in Tucson for the weather. At one time, we had four retired pastor couples.

Our high school group was very active. During the summer of 1973, we went up to Keams Canyon on the Navajo reservation. We would stay in the church's multipurpose room, which had a kitchen and recreation room. Our purpose for being there was to teach the reservation children at Vacation Bible School. We study and prepared for weeks before going, it was a wonderful experience for them as well as us.

To get the children from the reservation to the church, we would pick them up in an open bed truck. *What an experience.* We went out to where they had hogans made out of wood and mud that they lived in. It was an amazing lesson to learn that not everyone has a house, running water, a bathroom, or a car. It was so primitive and truly gave us much to appreciate. The whole experience was awesome. There were three chaperons and ten high school students. We would do this for three summers for a week at a time. It was an amazing time in our lives.

One of the other awesome things I loved about being in a church family was summer camp. We would go to the Tonto Rim Christian Camp every summer while growing up. When I was too old to attend as a student, I became a counselor. When I was in high school, I rededicated my life to following Jesus up at Tonto Rim, a life-changing experience. In future years, I would be the director of women's camps, and I would love it.

1974

For a month during the summer of 1974, I went to live with my maternal grandparents in Baltimore, Maryland. What an adventure I had. My grandparents, Nana and Papa, were great. Over the years, they had come to visit a couple of times. One time when my dad was in Vietnam, they drove across the United States and stayed with the five kids so my mom could go to Hawaii and have a vacation with my dad for rest and relaxation.

Nana had a speech impediment because she had strokes, starting when she was fifty years old, so she stuttered. She had always been in a servant role for Papa. She was a huggable, lovable woman who weighed three-hundred pounds and was only five foot four. Quite a difference from Papa, who was six-foot-four.

I had heard many stories about them, mainly that Papa had been a fireman, putting out fires on boats in the harbor for over twenty years. He was very opinionated and a racist, so much so that, even though my brother was getting married later that year, I was not supposed to mention that the best man was an African American. My mom said her dad would be furious.

I never have understood racism. I grew up going to school on military bases, and we have all nationalities and cultures attending together.

While in Baltimore, my papa had put up a chain-link fence around the backyard. I was his helper, but it should have been a guy or at least a stronger person than me. You had to make a hole in the ground to put the post in and then add cement. Next, you attach the fence to one end and pull the wire tight to the next post. It was incredibly hard, but we got it done.

Another great memory from that trip was I learned how to make the best cheesecake ever in a spring form pan. I still make the killer cheesecake. The month went quickly. I enjoyed my time in Baltimore; everything was so different than the desert of Arizona.

When I returned from Baltimore, I needed to get my hair trimmed for my senior picture. I went to a beautician and told her I wanted one to two inches cut off to even out my hair. When she finished, she had cut off six inches. I was so mad. I couldn't believe it. I cried and cried. There wasn't anything anyone could do, so I had to accept it. I decided no one would ever cut my hair again. Fortunately, my sister was going to beauty school, and soon I would only have her as my hairstylist.

AMERICAN BIRTHMARKS

Year		*Births*
1936	Post-Depression Slump	2,355,000
1946	Post-World War II Baby Boom Begins	3,411,000
1957	Baby Boom Peak	4,308,000
1973	Low Point Since 1946	3,137,000
1980	Birth Rate Turns Up	3,598,000
1985	Prediction (by US Census Bureau)	4,013,000

***

1975

In June 1975, I graduated from Catalina High School. I only had half days during my senior year, and I worked at Cecil Dooley Exterminator after my morning classes. I worked in the office, setting up appointments and doing the accounting. I learned how it was to work for a strict owner who was a perfectionist.

I attended Pima Community College and received a scholarship to cover the cost for two years. I graduated in June 1977 with two associates degrees: business management and business marketing.

I have struggled my whole life with self-doubt and depression. I think I should have been on medication, I had been taken to counselors and diagnosed as obese, but nothing ever seemed to help me. I could cry at the drop of hat and was a mess. It was after a crying spell that my mother said, "I think it is time for you to move out and see what is important."

When my mom suggested I move out, I started looking for options. I was attending the Vineyard Christian Fellowship, and I asked several girls if they needed a roommate. I found out that the Vineyard had a house they let single women move into. It would only be for a year, but it seemed like the best opportunity for someone moving out of their mom's and dad's home to a new home filled with single Christian women. I applied and was approved to move in.

The hostel home, as it was called by the Vineyard Christian Fellowship, was shared by five Christian women. We shared all house chores, cleaning, cooking, etc. We had weekly Bible studies and prayed together. I would share a room with Kathy, she was a few years older than me, but it was a good fit. We started behaving like sisters.

1978

My roommate's father was an ambassador to Chad in Africa. She was planning a trip to visit her parents in Africa by way of Paris. This is probably one of the few regrets I have in my life. She had asked me to go, it would only be five-hundred dollars. I asked my parents to loan me the money, but they said no and that it wouldn't be wise to borrow from a bank with how little I was making working in the family business. I didn't go, and to this day, I regret that I wasn't more assertive about what I wanted to do.

The year quickly passed and I needed to find a new place to live. Kathy and I decided to find an apartment that we could share. Kathy attended the University of Arizona to get a master's in business administration. She is so intelligent, she aced every test. Truly a brilliant woman.

We found a one-bedroom apartment not far from the hostel and it had the bus route Kathy used to attend school. It had a pool and Laundromat, too. It would be small, but we could do it. We had the guys at the Vineyard move us, we didn't have much, so it didn't take too long to get settled. We decided to split the refrigerator down the center to keep our food separate. Kathy was low on funds, so she would eat some of my food. This seemed to be the best way to keep track of what was whose.

Kathy's grandmother lived in Tucson, and she wanted to take me to meet her. She was a dignified woman, and she had an African American housemaid named Lucy. We came for dinner one night and we were instructed to ring a bell to let Lucy know if we needed anything. Grandma rang the bell and out came Lucy, saying, "Yes, Mama." This was a new world I had never been privy to.

My grandpa and grandma lived in Kearny for many years. My grandpa was a carpenter by trade, and he had built their house upon the Kearny Mining property. My grandparents later would move their house down from Kearny, which was on a hill, down to Winkelman flats. The flats were close to the Gila River, which was known to flood periodically. They moved the entire house on a flatbed truck down the hill to their new home in Winkelman. They put the house on big concrete bricks to hopefully protect their home in the event of flooding.

But in 1980, came the one-hundred-year flood people were hoping never to see. It was horrible, the water still rose up to two feet inside the house, ruining all my grandmother's prized pictures and furniture. They spent many days cleaning and replacing the carpet and repainting walls. Thankfully, they had put their home on a dirt mound with an additional four feet of brick for extra height. The houses around theirs were not higher but put right on the dirt ground. Total loss. My grandparents were devastated. My mom felt that this was the beginning of them dying.

Relationships Before Marriage, 1980

My first *boyfriend* was David Mejia, I met him in first grade. We were besties, always walking together, holding hands, smiling, and loving life. My family relocated back to Tucson after my dad retired from the army. David and I were friends again, but he had chosen a different lifestyle than me. Unfortunately, he died of AIDS before he could graduate from Catalina High School in 1975.

When I think back to my single years, I assumed I'd never been asked out much. Although as I read through my diaries from that time, I did go out with a lot of guys. Maybe not as a *girlfriend* but definitely as friends. My diaries became like a lifeline to God. I wrote about everything. I knew I would someday want to read them as a reminder of who I was back then and what I had experienced. Many times, reading old entries was a reminder about how God brought me through many difficult times, proof that I was never alone!

> *God is with you, wherever you may go and no matter what life brings. 1 John 5:4*

There were many times I would like different guys and couldn't think about much else. I guess I was guy crazy. I constantly would pray for God to give me peace about a special guy and give me an understanding of why I didn't have a serious boyfriend. I desperately wanted to date, get married, and start a family. In retrospect, I think it was good that I didn't date much because I might have married the first man to come along, even if it wasn't who God had planned for me. I had been to one of my girlfriend's wedding parties, and I was oh, so envious. I'm grateful that most of the guys just liked me as a friend.

My diary shows how I continually reflected on myself when some guy didn't do what I wanted, like call or ask me out. I would ask, "What is wrong with me? Why can't I have a boyfriend?" It made me feel like I was less than other girls my age. My self-worth was very low during that time. The feeling of rejection from guys brought up my insecurities, I never felt like the special person God had created. Which is clearly wrong because I had so many boys as friends. I hardly was home alone sulking. I was out having fun.

Not being able to see God's will for my life is what's best for me and in many cases, would prove to be so much better than I could have expected.

In April 1980, I wrote: "*The Lord is not here to grant my every wish! I am here to glorify God, to glorify Him, not to get everything I want. I am a sinner and only by the grace of God do I have eternal life. That is what is important. My life on earth is so short compared to the eternal time I'll have in heaven. The earthly things are not anything compared to what I'll have in my future. I need to serve God—that should be my focus, on serving Him. Knowing Him, seeking Him, building my relationship with Him, NOT seeking to please myself but bringing glory to God. God knows everything about me, all the good and the bad. Any blessings God brings me will be the fringe benefits—boyfriend, husband, children, etc.*"

On one occasion, I wrote: "*Oh well, I think that I've finally resigned myself to wait upon the Lord. Because it just isn't going to be right until the Lord brings my Mr. Right into my life.*"

Another entry: "*I think I'm finally at the point to say I'd rather be single if there isn't anyone that the Lord brings into my life. I'm better off with just myself and the Lord.*" That was written only six short months before I met my husband, Michael. The time that I waited seemed like an eternity. I was only twenty-two years old and had my whole life ahead of me. In retrospect, I should have just been grateful for the life I had; I've always been blessed with great friends and a wonderfully supportive family. I shouldn't have been so focused on finding someone. I wish I could have just trusted God and let Him do His work. I would have saved a lot of time and energy and, of course, tears.

In my college years, I had very high morals because I was raised in a strong Christian home. I planned to be a virgin when I married my husband. A couple of times, I had to defend my beliefs to others. I was involved heavily in Christian programs like Campus Crusade for Christ during my college days. On weekends, I attended a Christian fellowship called The Vineyard. We were all great friends; we could talk about everything. I loved being in those groups.

I also did quite a bit of traveling with friends. In September 1980, I planned a trip with a couple of my friends to go to San Francisco. I was so excited—one friend lived in Tucson and the other one lived in Montana. We wanted to see all the sights: Alcatraz, Muri Woods, Napa Valley, Monterey, Golden Gate Bridge, Sausalito, and Berkley. Oh, and we didn't want to forget the trolley cars, Ghirardelli Square, and Chinatown. We planned on staying for an entire week and keeping busy the whole time.

Before we left on our trip, I was working at the family business. On this particular day, I was in a bad mood. I had a bandage on the tip of my nose where a mole was removed, and I wasn't feeling good. That's when I turned around and saw a customer walking in.

He looked around and asked about Darth Vader accessories. I started to show him what we had, and he started to flirt with me. I was very attracted to him, and it became obvious that he liked me. He had a smile that could pierce through you. He was in town for a chess tournament, but he lived in Berkley, California, just across the bay from San Francisco. I told him that in a couple of weeks I was headed to San Francisco. He said, "Really? Here is my card when you get into San Francisco give me a call."

I was so excited, I couldn't wait to call and make a date. That's exactly what I did once we settled into our hotel room. I was so nervous to call him. A woman answered; I asked her if she could tell Don where I was staying and the hotel room I was in. She said she would. So, I waited. Sure enough, he called, and we made plans for him to pick me up and go to the Golden Gate Bridge park. He said he would bring his guitar to play while we sat in the park near a lake.

"Oh, how romantic," I thought. Thinking back on this story, I am reminded of a joke from the Hostel House that I lived in at the time: *Do you know how to have a "rotic" evening? It's having a romantic evening without the man.* We made up the name because there were only women sitting in front of the fireplace.

Don picked me up just outside of the hotel. He had a blue van. After a minute of small talk, I asked him who the woman on the phone was, the one who answered the phone.

"Oh, she's my wife," he replied.

Are you kidding me? Boy do I have lousy luck. He told me that they were in an open marriage, meaning they could have relationships with anyone they wanted. I was quick to tell him that I have very strong morals, and I was going to be a virgin when I married my future husband. He asked if there was anything he could do to change how I felt, but I said, *"No!"* However, we both agreed that we wanted to spend the day together, so off to the park we went.

It truly was a beautiful day. We sat on a blanket near the lake while we ate the lunch he had prepared. He periodically played me songs on his guitar and sang. Between singing and eating, we discussed subjects that interested both of us. Don asked me again if I was sure about going back into the van with him. Again, I declined his advances. He promised he would never do anything to hurt me, that he never ever wanted to hurt me.

I just smiled at him and said, "I know." It is weird how I had no fear of him hurting me although I had only met him once before. I felt peaceful. He told me to stop looking at him with my big blue beautiful eyes. I wondered… how many women had gone with him into the van?

Just think, I had been looking for someone to be affectionate and attentive to me. I had both right in front of me, but my standards and morals won out. They were more important than a fling in the park. Thanks to Jesus, I was given the strength to be strong in my faith and my morals. The day was an experience I will never forget. And what an ego booster!

Don said when he first met me, he knew that someday we would become lovers. I asked if he was serious. He said, "*Yes*." He believed with some people you can tell when you have chemistry. He believed we were soulmates, and he also said at the end of the day that he wanted to get together again before I left.

But I said, "Oh no, I don't want to be tempted and play with fire."

The last thing he said as he dropped me off was, "Just think, when I'm forty and you're thirty-three, we'll both be lying in bed laughing about this." Thank you, Don, for respecting me and giving me one of my favorite memories that I experienced before I was married.

A prayer I wrote to God, written in May 1980:

"Oh Lord, I want to seek You, to know You better. Lord,
I want to give my whole life to You every
corner, every room, every part of me.
Totally and not hold anything back for myself.
I want You to do with my life what is best for Jackie Lown.

Take me where You want me, show me what You want me to see,
guide me to where You want me to go.
Show me what my purpose, my mission in life is.
Where You want me to go and serve You.
Lord, help me to open my eyes to what spiritual gifts You
have blessed me with. Lord, I pray You will bind Satan
to stop attacking me every time I turn around.
I am a child of God who is here to love You and carry out Your will!
Praise God!
Thank You, God, that You have brought me to a
place of total commitment and total serenity
to follow you. No more falling into the hands of Satan.
But I only want to seek You and praise You.
Send Your angels to protect me from all things
that might hinder my Spiritual growth.
I just want to be totally content and not seek any worldly things.
Praise You, Lord, for Your patience and guidance!
Lord, work on my heart and my desires. I pray that You
change my desires away from worldly things.
Lord, they can only be changed by You; I thank You
that You have changed them. All glory to You.
I praise You and thank You, Lord, for the
friends You have brought into my life;
You have blessed me so much Lord, and I thank You for that.
I praise You, Lord, because You are such a
great Father, I love you, Lord.
I thank You, Jesus, that You died for my tears and my heartaches
and for Your work on me to make me the strong Christian woman
that You want me to be. Praise to You, Lord! Thank you, God!

My Marriage, 1982

What can I say about the man I have been married to since 1982? On the positive side, he is loving, funny, smart, kind, giving, a great caretaker, salesman, and a God-loving man. On the negative side, he is pessimistic, insecure, negative, impatient, and self-centered. He wants to be heard.

He was raised by his mother and grandmother. Michael's dad was fifty-five and his mom was thirty-five, so he was born very late in their lives. Michael's dad was an alcoholic, which upset the whole family. His family has stories about his dad watching him and putting the baby seat on the counter at a bar while he drank. It wasn't a happy time for Michael's mother. Needless to say, they split due to the problem. His father left when Michael was two years old, never to be seen again.

I've said this many times: Michael's saving grace was literally his grandmother named Grace. She was old school and raised Michael as her own. She was very strict, although Michael has stories about how he played his mom against his grandmother to get the result that he wanted. He usually got his way and was very good at manipulation. One time he was told to cut the grass, but he didn't think the lawn needed it. To get around doing the chore, he started up the lawnmower and left it in one spot. After a bit, he moved it to the side of the house. He repeated this until he had gone around the whole house, making grandma Grace think he finished mowing.

Grandma Grace was the reason Michael learned how to take care of a girl, which has benefitted me greatly. She also taught him to be a great cook. This has kept us weight-challenged our whole marriage.

His mother was a nurse and worked nights, so Michael did not see her very often. She was always ill with gastric issues, taking too many pills to try to deal with her pain. I wonder how much of her pain was from illness or from a broken heart. She always seemed to talk about Michael's dad lovingly but knew it wasn't good to raise a boy around that lifestyle. During Michael's childhood, his mother became addicted to painkillers. She was sent to a hospital in Phoenix to dry out and recover from them. Michael told me that she was mad at him and blamed him for her problems. It is a terrible thing to blame an innocent young child. Due to Michael's family dynamics, he has always had a victim mentality with people. That is such a hard thing to try to overcome, I'm not sure if it is possible.

I met Michael in October 1980. My girlfriend and I had decided to start attending a larger church than the one we had been going to and one closer to the university, hoping there would be an abundance of college-aged guys. I decided one Sunday to go to the evening service. And there he was, sitting five rows away from me. Tall, handsome, great smile, curly brown hair with a big barrel chest, and hopefully single. I did something I had never done before; after the service was over, I walked up to him and said, "I don't believe I've met you." That's all it took, we were inseparable after that. He asked me to join his Sunday school class at a diner after the service, and I accepted.

I worked at the family costume shop and had season tickets to the University of Arizona football games since we took care of their mascots, Wilma and Wilber Wildcat. During the social time, it came up that he loved football. Ah, now I had an "in." Afterward, he walked me to my car, and I asked him if he wanted to go with me to the Notre Dame Football game this coming week. He agreed and our first date was set.

It was a memorable time. I learned very quickly that he was not a sharer. He went to get us snacks, and I said we could share a drink. He told me does *not* share food with anyone. I came from a family of seven, where we shared everything. Michael told me that the first time he came over to my parents' house, my dad had an ice cream container that he passed around with one spoon to share. I never thought about that being something others didn't do, that was how I was raised! But Michael, being an only child, was very different. He was grossed out about it.

We only dated three months when Michael popped the question. He asked me in a very original way. I didn't realize how this would resonate with our whole marriage.

He asked, "Will you marry me?" and I said, "Yes!"

"Does this mean I should start saving for my wife's hip surgeries?"

He likes to say he had strep throat and was on his death bed when he proposed. He *was* sick but not dying.

We were married on March 20, 1982, fifteen months after he proposed. If I had to do it over, I would not want to have such a long engagement. It is very difficult to stick to your morals and wait to be intimate until you're married when you are so attracted to each other and filled with love.

Once, we were lying on the floor listening to Kenny Rogers, just being in each other's arms. Suddenly, I felt him undoing my bra. *"What?"* I thought. "This can't be happening!" I was furious; I told him I couldn't believe that he did that, and he needed to leave right now. I felt strongly about my morals and wasn't going to waver. We made up shortly after that, and he never tried it again.

One of the reasons our wedding didn't happen right after the engagement was because of the events that transpired on Valentine's Day in 1981. A robber had broken into the house I was renting. I lived with my best friend Kara, who worked nights as a nurse, and her father, who was my landlord. I slept at one end of the house, and she and her dad slept at the other end. Luckily, her father had woken up and scared the intruder away. Oh, I was so thankful that I slept through it all.

When my best friend came home in the morning, I told her about the excitement. She asked where my car was and I was dumbfounded. My car should have been parked right outside my room where I could see it through my plate glass window. I opened up my curtain to see, and my white Pinto was gone!

While I was sleeping, the robber came into my room and lifted the car keys off my desk. I kept my keys right next to my head. It was unbelievable that I slept soundly through it all. My purse was still there, but the cash was gone and now so was my car. I worked at the family business and made very little. With my car gone, I had to bike to work. Thankfully, it was only a couple of miles from where I lived. But now Michael and I had to postpone the wedding because we needed to save money.

I have always been a very sound sleeper. Once, when I was in an Ecumenical youth group in high school, we went to a retreat on Mount Lemmon. We went up on a Friday and planned to stay through Monday. We were in this huge cabin that had a kitchen and a fireplace but no separate rooms for sleeping. Everyone slept everywhere, all thirty of us. I thought it would be hard to miss anything while we were all together. But I woke up Sunday morning and asked where a certain girl was. I had gotten to know her, but I didn't see her anywhere. The others acted shocked that I didn't know where she was. She and some others went running outside during the evening, and she'd fallen off a cliff. The search and rescue team came out to find her and took her in a helicopter to Tucson Medical Center. Thankfully, she was okay, only badly bruised. They said there was so much noise that they didn't understand how I slept through the whole thing. I don't know either. It's crazy to think anyone could sleep through such noise and commotion. But I did.

Back to the love of my life: Michael and I first chose the date for our wedding—September 1981, but when my car was stolen, as I mentioned earlier our wedding date was pushed back because we needed to save money. Having a seasonal family business meant I needed to work from October through New Year's Day. We decided that after Easter, we would have a beautiful spring wedding. On Saturday, March 20, 1982, we were married. The first day of spring.

I had always wanted to make my wedding dress with my mom and have my dad bead its bodice. He had spent his whole life working with different beads to recreate American Indian lore and mountain man handiwork. So, with the date now so far in the future, that could happen. I didn't think anything could make me happier than to be married and start my life with Michael.

I think back now to all the times where I desperately wanted to find "Mister Right" and spent hours crying to the Lord about it, wasting so much time! I look back and think, "Why couldn't I just be relaxed in the Lord and trust He would do what He said?"

> *I will be with you. I will not leave you nor forsake you... The Lord your God is with you wherever you go. Joshua 1:5, 9*

> *Wait on the Lord; be of good courage, and He shall strengthen your heart; wait, I say, on the Lord! Psalm 27:14*

A couple of days before our wedding, we needed to pick up Michael's mom from Phoenix. We had a small window of four hours to do it. Rehearsal at the church started at five p.m. and dinner was at six-thirty p.m. We arrived at her home thinking we would pick her up and go right back to Tucson, but she didn't have anything to wear to the wedding.

"Really?" I thought. "We've only been engaged a year and a half. It's not like you didn't have time to get something." Frantically, we found a plus-size shop and got her a beautiful dress to wear. Back in the car, she said she needed new shoes. We both replied that what she was wearing would work perfectly and rushed back to Tucson.

As we tried to get on the freeway, it was already three p.m. and we were in wall-to-wall traffic. I was in the back seat, Michael was trying to stay calm, and his mother said loudly, "Why doesn't that guy get his head out of his..."

I had only met her a couple of times before now and I, being the naive little Christian girl I was, was speechless. My eyes must have looked like quarters. Michael looked at me in his rearview mirror and was also bug-eyed.

"Wow, this was going to be interesting," I thought. We made it in time, although we were a little rattled.

Our wedding was on a beautiful spring day. My extended family was all in attendance. It couldn't have been better!

Our honeymoon was a wonderful experience with fun memories. The first night together, we stayed at the Double Tree Inn on Alvernon Way in Tucson. Michael made the mistake of telling his best man where we were going to stay, so he and his wife went to the hotel room and short-sheeted the bed, and put plastic wrap on the toilet. I thought it was hilarious but Michael was furious. He went and complained to the management, asking why they would let anyone in our room. That definitely made it memorable. The next day, we saw our car had been sprayed with shaving cream to say, "Don't be knocking if this truck is a rocking." And there was Limburger cheese stuffed in the tailpipe.

Our destination was Durango, Colorado, but we stopped in Flagstaff the next night and stayed at Little America. Then we headed to Durango by way of the Four Corners. We stayed in the Historic Strater Hotel in the honeymoon suite. We took a train ride to Silverton and went on the ski lifts. There wasn't enough snow to ski, but it was a fun time. There was a Rocky Mountain Chocolate Factory where we got some chocolate candy to enjoy. After going to the movies, we went back to the hotel to sleep.

Not being used to sleeping with anyone, I rolled over in the queen-sized bed (mind you, neither of us were very small) and hit Michael's left eye with my elbow. He jumped up and ran to the bathroom to look at his eye, all the while I apologized profusely. He came back to bed with his hand covering his eye and then showed me his eye, it was already black and blue.

"*Oh no*! All of our pictures were going to show his black eye," I thought. As I was feeling terrible about hitting him, he started cracking up. In the bathroom, he used my makeup and colored his eye to look bruised. It was a hysterical prank. We laughed and laughed.

That was just the beginning of our trip. We rode the train to Silverton, Colorado, and Michael took forty pictures of the gorge there, only to find out that they all looked the same after we had them developed. Michael had never seen anything like the gorge. It was beautiful. Everywhere we looked there were pine trees and down at the bottom of the gorge we saw a creek, running with clear water. He had never seen such beauty before and wanted to ensure we had a good picture to save.

On our way home, we stopped by the Petrified Forest National Park. We talked about superstitions, about the bad things that would happen to anyone who took any pieces of wood. I told Michael not to take any wood.

We stayed at a small hotel. It was cold and raining, and Michael wanted to bring a small kitten inside. It had been outside in the rain. As he tried to turn on the sink to get the kitten some water, the handle broke off and cut him. This alarmed me enough to ask if he had taken any petrified wood, but he told me no. Then, forgetting that he was allergic to cats, he began having trouble breathing.

I asked again, "Did you take any petrified wood?" As I inquired, his eyes were already starting to close. I asked a third time, and the truth came out. "Yes," he said. "And tomorrow we will be taking it back!" That was only the beginning of a humorous union.

Once we were married, we decided that we wanted to spend our first years of marriage getting to know each other and build a home. When it was time to start a family, we would. The only thing we hadn't planned on was being infertile. Three years after our wedding, we started trying with no success, nothing. During this time, I repeated my doubt and fear that I would never have a baby. Oh, how time was wasted again. We finally decided to look into infertility testing.

Infertility, 1986

The first time I worried about being infertile was in college. My best friend and roommate, Kara, was attending nursing school. She said in a matter of fact way that I was probably infertile because I had undergone an excessive amount of X-rays. I rejected her thinking. *No, not a chance. I was going to have tons of kids*. But the thought never left me after she introduced the possibility.

Little did I know how true her statement would turn out to be! When Michael and I were married, I stayed on birth control pills so I wouldn't get pregnant before we wanted to have a child. Turns out, I never needed to worry about that happening because I was not fertile. When we decided we were ready to start "trying," we had been married three years. It was a long two years of trying with no results.

I thought infertility was something I would never experience. I imagined being a fertile, happy mother to many children. It's heartbreaking to find out that dreams I had growing up could never happen. It was time to look into our options.

After being depressed for months, we decided to go to a fertility doctor. The doctor ran many tests to see if there were any underlying issues. They monitored us for a couple of months before we could get started on any medications. Michael went to a urologist, and they found that his white blood cell count was too high, which in turn lowered his healthy sperm count. (Michael joked that he only needed one, right?) I was found to have immature eggs because of how many X-rays I had undergone, and my body wasn't producing enough healthy viable eggs. The day they found out about my immature eggs, they told me I was ovulating and it was a good day to try and get pregnant with *viable* sperm. But the doctor was clear, with both of our issues, there was *no way* we could get pregnant without their help. They wanted to start both of us on medication the following month that would help increase Michael's sperm count and help my eggs get to maturity.

I was devastated! I went to work and cried to my mom. I couldn't believe it, no children without medical help. Oh, I was so upset.

But God had a plan. At that time, I could not see any farther than the doctor's diagnosis. But like usual, God had a master plan way better than anything we could ever plan out ourselves.

My mother tried to console me and thought about how she could help.

Out of the blue, she said, "What excites Michael?"

I replied, "He loves anything black."

We both thought for a minute. This was in 1987 and Elvira was hot. *What a great idea*! I could dress up like her. I put on one of the costume shop's slinky black dresses that had a slit from the bosom down to the belly button and another slit that went up the thigh, much higher than anything I would ever normally wear. I put on a black wig with long black hair that was teased at the top to make it super high. And I didn't forget her whip! Who says God doesn't have a sense of humor? The doctor had said earlier in the day that I was ovulating and could get pregnant if everything went right for us.

Guess what? My period didn't come the next month. Around this time, the first home pregnancy test had just come out. I decided to give it a try, and the test said I was pregnant. We did it, we proved everyone wrong. We were pregnant!

I called the infertility clinic and told them what had happened with the home test. "That can't be," the clinic told me. "You two don't have what it takes to create a viable fetus. Or you could have a hysterical pregnancy."

I thought, "What? No, don't be a downer. I believe the test and I'm not faking it!" I was instructed to come and give the clinic a blood sample to confirm.

The nurse who did my blood test said she couldn't believe it, but I was pregnant. However, it was considered a high-risk pregnancy. I took daily pregnancy vitamins and had estrogen added to my vagina so I wouldn't miscarry. I was very excited and willing to do whatever I needed to do to keep the baby. I went to the ob-gyn appointments and constantly was reminded I was at high risk. I followed everything I was supposed to do.

October 1987 was, as usual, a crazy Halloween. It was my first Halloween as an owner of the costume shop, and I wanted to be there through the end of Halloween.

It was time for my seven-month checkup, and my doctor said, "You have high blood pressure, and your legs are swelling. You must get off your legs and be in bed for the next two months."

I was crushed. I longed to be working at my new business, but the baby had to come first. I pretty much kept off my legs until it was delivery time.

By the end of December, I went to see my doctor, and he said my baby was getting too big. I needed to pick a date to be induced. Christmas was in two days, and my first thought was to have his birthday on a separate day so he could have it to himself to celebrate. We decided to induce the baby at six a.m. on December 28.

On that day, we were at the hospital at five a.m. The doctor broke my water and said it wouldn't take too long. But the day dragged on and the baby wasn't coming. The nursery waiting room was filled with our family. It was awesome, but I became tired and questioned when our much-wanted baby would arrive.

It became obvious that our baby was bigger than anticipated, and we were going to need help. It was a difficult birth. It took a man on each side of me, pressing on my stomach, to get the baby out. They performed an episiotomy and used forceps, too. My baby was ten pounds and healthy, but his poor little head came out swollen.

When it came to name our new Lown-Peters family member, I was sure we were having a little girl. I made a deal with Michael that he could name our child if we had a boy, and I would name our child if we had a girl. Being as sure as I was about us having a girl, I wanted to name her Sarah Nicole. I felt this was a good bet. I surely would win. But the day came, and I was wrong.

My husband wanted to choose an unusual name because he felt his own name was too common, and he disliked that wherever he was, there was often another person named Michael. If I had the chance to name our child, I (having a uniquely spelled name) would choose a normal name. Our precious baby boy was named Skyler Benjamin Lown-Peters. We chose Benjamin after my great-grandfather. We were so excited and couldn't love him more than we already did!

We started 1988 as a family of three. We were so blessed to have this happy, perfect ten-pound bouncing baby boy.

My Career, 1987

"Don't get your identity from your job. Don't make your career your life. Let it be your passion, let it bring you pleasure, but don't let it become your identity; you are so much more valuable than that."
–Celine Dion

I believe before starting your career, learn to build your foundations, learn your likes and dislikes, don't ever be afraid to express them. If you can realize you are capable of many things, you'll be able to survive anything life throws at you.

I had a dream job growing up. I knew I wanted to be in charge of something. But what? My sister dreamt of being a hairdresser—hence all my Barbie dolls were bald because she cut and styled their hair. I only knew that I wanted to get married and have lots of kids. So I learned how to cook and clean and do laundry, all the motherly things. But everything changed when my dad retired from the Army and we moved from Fort Huachuca, Arizona to Tucson, Arizona.

My mother started sewing for a small costume shop down in South Tucson. With her love of costumes and reenactments, it was a great fit. When the owner closed the shop, she saw that there was a need to be filled, and my mom and dad opened a costume shop in the middle of Tucson. My dad was working his first civilian job in a long time at a local hospital. He started as the security manager, then they added a print shop and several other departments. Soon, it was too much work. He was retired and didn't need to work so hard. The costume shop was doing great and needed more help, so shortly after my dad quit the hospital, he became a full-time business owner with my mom.

Practically right after the store was opened, I started working there after high school. I helped customers, worked on costume creation, and managed the store when my parents were gone. I knew someday that I would be the proud owner of our shop—Lown's Costumes, Inc. For nearly thirty-five years, we had our family business, something that would bring joy and heartache many times over.

Once I knew I wanted to take over the shop, the opportunity came quicker than I expected. In 1986, after the craziness of Halloween, my parents came to me to see if Michael and I wanted to buy the store from them. My parents were tired of the day-to-day operations and the craziness of Halloween. The store had become a treasure to Tucson. We had lines of people wrapping down and around our business just to come in and see what we had. It was awesome, our family turned all focus to the business to keep it a success.

In 1987, my dad stepped away from the everyday activities of the costume shop and became the most honored docent at the Historical Society. He went to many middle schools to teach about Southwest history, dressing the part, and taking along the items that would resemble actual tools of the day.

He was also very active in the Tucson Vigilantes and the Tucson Jaycee's, where he was the chief officer and active member for many years. In the early days when you could go to airports without many restrictions, he and the members would go to the airport dressed in their Western garb and "hang" dignitaries who were coming to Tucson, making their arrival a very memorable experience. He also headed up many events to welcome travelers where he would ride with a sheriff up and down I-10 and pull over any couples who looked like they could stay for a week during the Tucson Rodeo activities. These lucky couples received anything they needed, all expenses were paid by local Tucson businesses. Many of the club's Rodeo Parade floats were designed and created by my dad.

Another club he was involved in was the Tucson Mountain Men Association, making and wearing leather outfits to look the part. He bought a teepee and traveled to many reservations across the country, enjoying reenacting history. He loved dressing up. In the costume shop's early days, he had a full department selling mountain man supplies like beads, tomahawks, books, and leather.

He also gave acting a try, signing with Folse Talent Agency, which got him several commercials. One gig was with Eegee's, a local sandwich joint, and another gig was a small part in the movie *Billy the Kid*. For the movie, he was originally in the back as an extra in the court scene, but he looked so good that he was moved to the front row.

His other costumed fun was to play Santa for all of the grandchildren who lived here in Tucson. He quickly became Grandpa HoHo to them.

When the opportunity to buy the costume shop from my parents came, I wanted to jump in with both feet. At the time, there was no thinking about it. It was destiny for me to become the owner. Now, many years later, I realize I should have slowed down and sought God's direction. This was what I wanted, but it wasn't what my mother wanted. I didn't realize that this would cause trouble in the future. Could you argue that if it was of God, would it have lasted twenty more years? I don't know, I just wanted to be in charge and make it a success.

We had moved the store to another location, and it became very obvious that the Internet and all the satellite costume stores were threatening our business.

Post-Traumatic Stress Disorder

After the birth of Skyler, my oldest son, I had postpartum depression and started weekly counseling sessions.

If my accident had happened in the late seventies, I believe my family and I would have been put in counseling to deal with all the dysfunction that it caused.

Through counseling, I wanted to learn why I felt *less* than everyone else. All I wanted to do was cry and be sad. I had wanted to have a baby for so long—my whole life, in fact. Why, then, was I so unhappy? I wondered, "Is it because of the accident and having special needs?"

This is a journal entry from 1988:

> *When I hit [rock] bottom, I feel as though God is not there. I feel as though I am alone and don't understand what is going on around me. I somehow missed in my growing years the truth. That God is in my heart. Deep within my heart, with me! ALWAYS! I somehow felt that God is out there far away, in the clouds, in the sky, [a] man in the moon mentality. I know He is alive but, somehow, I did not feel it personally. That is my hope, that I can come to believe that He is a part of me and here to help me when I*

> *need help. I can call on Him. I want to daily turn my life over to Jesus and trust that His will be done and that He would show me the path to take. I want to be able to say when times get hard that I will cling to Jesus with all on my heart and mind and soul and trust that God is in control and truly feel blessed that I am who I am and that I am so fortunate to have such a wonderful husband and son. It is only by the Grace of God that I have come through this year. With my feet on the ground and being able to handle the things that I have had to handle, I thank the Lord for guiding me to my counselor to help me work through my childhood memories and see that I am a beautiful, strong woman.*

I learned quite a lot about myself and how my brain works through all the counseling sessions. Part of the counseling was in group therapy once we went on a weekend up to Mount Lemmon to be in cooler weather. The counseling was intense, I learned what my triggers are and how they cause me flashbacks—consciously or subconsciously. It is amazing how the human brain works.

My post-traumatic stress disorder (PTSD) was diagnosed through my counselors. Just recently, I was diagnosed with CPTSD, a new diagnosis for PTSD. The C stands for chronic. With all the military PTSD, medical professionals have been reclassifying titles and distinguishing between certain symptoms.

I can quickly be thrown into the past. I have fainted while visiting someone in the hospital just from the smells and seeing the patients. If I'm in front of a car pulling into a parking space, just the motion of the car heading toward me will make me turn white and weak. I know not to cross in front of cars. While pumping gas, I can smell the ether fumes, which send me back to the operating table. Ether is what was used in the sixties to put patients to sleep for surgery.

The triggers are real and I still struggle with them all today. Feeling vibrations is especially bad around construction sites that use vibrating tools like jackhammers. It makes my skin crawl, and I will leave immediately to get away from it. This trigger stems from having my body casts removed. If you have never had a cast removed, they use a small rotary saw and usually go up the sides of the cast to make it easier to separate. The blade isn't so sharp that it would cut your skin, but it vibrates and is loud. Hearing or feeling vibrations unearths an immediate unconscious memory.

For one Halloween, I wore a Raggedy Ann costume that had stocking material for the arms and legs. I was going crazy wearing it but didn't know why until many years later. The stocking material used to cover the arms and legs was the same type of material used to cover skin before a cast is put on.

My triggers don't stop there. Another one I have is bright white sheets like you might find at a hotel. My mind subconsciously thinks I am in a hospital bed. Thankfully, I learned to label the triggers and be in charge of them. When I acknowledge them, they have less control over me.

It was explained to me that I have tried to combat the effects of PTSD by separating myself from my body. From my neck down, I don't acknowledge anything, including pain. I guess in some instances, that is good, but most of the time, I tune myself out from any discomfort or pain. I have worked on a broken foot for much too long before I saw a doctor.

One time, I was with my mother and she asked me what was wrong with my toe. I said, "Nothing, why?" only to look down and see that my big toe was inflamed. I went to the podiatrist the next day, and he said the toenail needed to be removed. Crazy! I have a high threshold for pain, but I truly believe I tune the pain out to the point of being injured way more than if I took care of the issue when the pain started.

Once I learned how to handle the PTSD episodes, my life became much more peaceful. It takes some forethought to acknowledge them when they are happening, but it's better to know what's going on than to be reacting and not know why.

If you have been through a traumatic experience in your life, I would encourage you to be checked out for this disorder. I am grateful I learned about my PTSD and was taught how to live with it.

My First Total Hip Replacement, 1989

I was under the understanding that all my hip surgeries up to this point were the only surgeries I was going to need. But when I was twenty, I soon found out that was not the case. I had to have annual appointments to keep track of my hip and to keep my pain level in check.

When I was twenty years old, I was at my annual doctor's appointment, getting X-rays. I was told that when I couldn't take the pain anymore, I would have a total hip replacement. I was in shock. I thought I was done having surgeries.

I talked with my doctor, and he said I should try to have my family before I have the surgery due to the stress childbirth places on hips. I quickly became enraged. After all, I felt betrayed because I thought I was done with surgeries. All I could do was cry because I was not looking forward to having any more. I asked my mom if she knew I needed more surgeries. She said yes, but both of my parents had decided not to tell me because I had gone through enough already. I know they had my best interest at heart, but I was hurt and distraught.

I put off thinking about it and focused on trying to be strong and healthy, monitoring everything that I did with my hip. I worried about it constantly.

I was married four years later, at twenty-four. I thought I had lots of time for children—no worries, right? Against all odds, I delivered a healthy ten-pound baby when I was thirty years old. I continued trying to delay my future hip replacement surgery by watching my weight-bearing but carrying a ten-pound baby around made it difficult. I had injections in the joint to kill the pain but that didn't last long. I did not want to have surgery, I wanted to put it off as long as possible.

Skyler was fifteen months old when I dislocated my right hip. I was watching TV and had just put him to bed. Michael was also sleeping when I plopped myself onto our family room couch. I felt an unspeakable pain and realized what had happened. I sat there for a while trying to figure out what to do. I called Michael but got no response. I called him for about fifteen minutes and didn't rouse him. I got myself onto the floor and crawled down the hall to our bedroom. I called to him again and finally, he shot right out of bed. He called 911 and asked if they could arrive without sirens on because our baby was asleep.

I was taken to Tucson Medical Center and put in surgery to reduce my hip. If they couldn't reset the hip, they would have to open it up and fix it. Luckily, my hip went right into the socket. I had to be careful for the next week and needed to see my doctor. After seeing Dr. Hugh Thompson III, he had been my doctor for it seemed like forever, he said we need to schedule hip replacement surgery as soon as possible.

In August of 1989, my total hip replacement was performed. I received an S-ROM prosthetic. It was different from other possible hip replacements since I was thirty-two and didn't have a normal hip socket to work with. My doctor had to use bone fragments from my femur bone to cement in my new hip. All I know is this surgery was the most painful surgery I had ever had. I woke up from this surgery with an IV in my neck because my veins were collapsing, and they couldn't find a viable vein. The IV was incredibly painful; I couldn't even turn my neck. I couldn't wait to get it out. The IV was attached to a machine which regulated my pain medications. If I needed some medicine, I just hit the button. It made me think I had control, but I believe it was all bogus, that it used predetermined intervals to administer the drugs.

I was in the hospital for two weeks to ensure that I started healing with no problem and to give me reprieve from the baby. I was lucky to be put in a private room during my long stay. The hospital made special allowances for me because my son was almost two years old, and they allowed him to come into my room to visit. Usually, children are not allowed into your room. I was very grateful that they allowed him in.

The chief operator of the hospital was a member of our church. He would put a single red rosebud in each room for patients he personally knew. I received a new one every couple of days. It was great because the nurses knew we were friends with the big boss, so they always treated me with great care.

During my stay at Tucson Medical Center, my physical therapy consisted of many exercises, including side lifts which hurt, so when I was offered water therapy, I jumped at the chance. To this day, I continue water therapy and find it very soothing, pain-free, and easier to do. It has become a real quiet time for me, and I miss it when I can't do it.

After the two weeks were over, I went home and found that Michael had rented a medical bed for the next three months for my convalescing. It was put in our family room so I would not have to get in and out of our tall waterbed. It was great! I like hospital beds because I can use the bar above my head to center myself or move up in the bed.

I was on crutches for three months after I was released, and I could only lightly touch my toe on the ground. After the doctor's visit at three months, I moved to a walker for an additional three months. After the walker, I moved to a cane. I asked the doctor how long it would be before I felt back to normal. The answer was at least a full year. And he was right, by one year, I was feeling pretty good. I didn't need to use a cane unless I had to walk long distances.

I have never liked using walkers or canes. Especially back then, they made me feel old, like a senior citizen. I think I despised them because no one gets out of the way. When I used motorized wheelchairs, like the kind you see at Walmart, people ignored me completely. I have found that people who have experience using these aids are the same people who help open doors and move out of the way. I realize these tools help me get back to being healthy, but I have struggled with them my whole life.

During my convalescing, Skyler was a fabulous helper. He was a big boy and quite tall for a two-year-old. He would help me carry things and pick up things for me, an amazing child. He always has been a happy person and a joy to have around.

After being home for about two months, I started to go stir crazy, I love to work, so I started slowly, going in part-time. The only problem was controlling Skyler and keeping him near me. No matter how great Skyler was, he was still a toddler and I was on a walker, which limited what I could do and hold. We bought a child leash for him. It allowed me to get Skyler into the car safely. When I took him to daycare, one of the caretakers would come out and get him from me, saving me from getting out of the car. We did this for about three months until I could walk him safely.

Our dogs at the time were two Chow Chows. Our male was called Max and our female was named Minnie. They were beautiful, our whole family loved them. We'd purchased Max locally but Minnie we bought while visiting friends in Oklahoma City. She was a female and had an attitude. We had just spent our Thanksgiving with family and were cleaning up when we heard Skyler scream out and start crying. He was holding a turkey leg that Minnie had gone for and bit Skyler on the nose. His face was covered in blood.

We rushed him to the ER, where they took great care of him. Since he was so young, he had to be strapped to a board while the doctor stitched his nose. Fortunately, we were able to get a plastic surgeon to do the stitching and the scar on his nose has disappeared entirely. Unfortunately, the dog had to be quarantined for two weeks, and we decided to find her a new home. We had hoped to breed them, but Max had a descended testicle and was unable to breed. The best thing was that Skyler wasn't traumatized by the experience. I think I was because I felt guilty. I hope to never experience anything like it again.

One night after putting Skyler to bed, I felt a sting on my foot as I walked through our kitchen. I had been stung by a scorpion. *Ouch!* I yelled out to Michael to come over. I told him to get a cup and take it with us to the ER, but he was flustered by the situation. Michael started to yell at me. This made me mad.

I said, "I'm the one who got bit. Calm down, I need you!" He did calm down and contacted my mom so she could come take care of Skyler. We went to the ER with the scorpion in a jar and my swollen, numb leg. I stayed there for four hours to be watched in case any other symptoms appeared and was given a shot. My leg stayed numb for a couple of days, but I had no problem recovering.

I was very grateful that Skyler wasn't up because he had just been in the kitchen. I was told that the smaller the scorpion, the stronger their venom is, and this one was small. It could have been deadly for him. God was protecting us. Praise the Lord!

My Nathan

Nathan means, "A gift from God."

When we had the healthy birth of Skyler, Michael and I felt so blessed. We no longer used protection, realizing that if we got pregnant, we would be doubly blessed. Little did we know what our future would hold.

I got pregnant again, and we were so excited but also cautious. My first visit to the ob-gyn was interesting. I explained that my first pregnancy was high risk and I thought he should prescribe the same medicine I had taken to give the fetus the best opportunity for survival. But he said all pregnancies are different and didn't believe I would need it. My mistake was respecting the doctor and not pressing for the medicine. I don't blame him, but it became our reality that I miscarried in my fifth month of pregnancy. I went through every emotion: anger, hate, depression. I didn't understand why this was happening. Our baby was gone.

Little did we know that God, our Lord and Master, was working behind the scenes. I miscarried in January 1992 at five months along. I spent the rest of the year in counseling, trying to understand and accept that I would never have another baby biologically.

I spoke with Michael about adoption, but he had no interest in adoption. He was an only child and saw nothing wrong with only having one child. I grew to respect his decision but did not agree. I grew up in a family with five children and dreamt of having a house full of children. Accepting that there were not going to be more children was next to impossible. Besides, I always wanted more children because a single child may not learn to share with others and may become selfish.

Our family business, which now was owned by Michael and me, was the focus of our life. I stayed busy and was responsible for running the business day-to-day. Michael would take the last two weeks of October off from his Holsum Bakery job each year to work the business. We would divide up the responsibilities, he worked the sales department and I worked in the rental department.

One of the practices of Lown's was to hire students from Catalina High School business classes for our fall season. We did that for over ten years, having great success educating and helping students who wanted to learn.

One of the students we employed changed our family forever. It was October 1992 when I hired a sweet, petite young lady. She worked through Christmas, and then she was done. I wouldn't see her again until September 1993. She came to share that she was pregnant and wanted Michael and me to adopt her baby.

She shared that she came from a family who did not want her. She had been sent to live with family members and never felt loved, a terrible feeling she never wanted her baby to experience. Although she knew the father, they had no relationship and he didn't want the baby. Abortion was not an option, so giving the baby up for adoption was her only choice. She believed she had been hired to work at our costume shop for a reason: to meet Michael and me to see how our loss had affected us, to learn how much we wanted to have another child.

You can't believe how excited I was! I was willing to adopt her and the baby I was so excited. She had only spoken to me, so I had the job of telling Michael this incredible news. As I said before, Michael didn't want to adopt. He immediately said no. He said

Skyler was getting to the point where he could take care of himself. Did I really want to start over with a baby? Of course, I said yes! It took him about a week to realize that this was a gift from God—how could he say no? It was going to happen. I was going to have another baby.

I was still seeing a counselor periodically and I shared with her this great news. She clearly stated that she thought it was a bad idea to have the birth mother involved with us in raising the child. It was decided through a counseling session with her that we would only be with her until the baby was born and then we would separate. I would send her a letter every birthday with an update of the baby's progress and health. She filled out a questionnaire about her health and things we might need to know while he grew up.

We hired an adoption lawyer who was an adoptee herself to guide us through the adoption process. We first had to get fingerprinted, and then had background checks, and finally had a home inspection for the state adoption. We had to follow several guidelines. We could buy the birth mother some clothes but could only give her one-hundred dollars. We could *not* buy the baby.

I drove the mother to all of her doctor's appointments. As with any pregnancy, in the beginning, her visits were monthly and as time went by, her visits became more frequent. I was thrilled to be a part of the appointments. One time, the doctor asked her if her baby was moving, and she pointed to me and said yes, the baby was moving.

It wasn't long until she needed clothes, so I took her to get some clothes. I bought her just a couple of outfits because she said that was all she needed. I, on the other hand, am a fashionista and love clothes. When I was born, I was my mom's first daughter. Her friends who had daughters a few years older than me had sent my mom their children's clothes they had outgrown. Between my mom being a seamstress and receiving hand-me-down clothes, my closet was always full of many choices, which I loved. My closet was always full, I had twenty different tops and dresses to wear when I was pregnant. Definitely too many, but she only wanted a couple of items, which seemed too minimalist.

Before we knew it, it was time for the baby to be born. I was called the moment that her water broke. I picked her up and Michael met us at the hospital. My sister Jodi babysat Skyler while we were away.

We were ready, the nursery was ready, and Skyler had been spoken to about us adopting the baby as a family. It wouldn't be only mom and dad adopting the baby, but him, too. He would have a little brother and all the responsibilities that came with that. Skyler was excited! We were ready to meet our new family member.

Michael and I waited in the delivery room for a long time. Something was wrong, the baby was not coming. The delivery doctor called for more assistance. The baby had the umbilical cord wrapped around his neck. Everyone was getting more and more concerned, but thankfully out came our blue baby boy. He was so blue from the umbilical cord being wrapped around his neck three times.

The nurses grabbed him and took him to the side incubator. We heard nothing. We knew that the baby needed to take a breath and that would produce a cry. There was nothing, not a sound. But all of the sudden, out came a whimpering cry. Michael and I looked at each other, fearing the worst. But our baby boy was alive and breathing. The doctor told us our baby was meant to be here because most babies can't handle the limited air they receive if they get wrapped up in the umbilical cord.

The greatest gift we received from this selfless girl was our beautiful baby boy, we named Nathan Andrew Lown-Peters. The only request from his birth mother was to have a moment with him before she left the hospital, which we honored. But Nathan was not officially ours yet. He was still the birth mother's and father's until their parental rights were relinquished. That caused a problem for me not being able to stay in the hospital with him. The nurses at the hospital were awesome because they kept him overnight until he was released. They let me stay in an unoccupied room to feed him and be with him.

I knew he was so special. While all the other babies were sleeping in the nursery, he was mesmerized by the lights above. He grew up fascinated with lights and has always been drawn to them.

It was two long weeks until we were able to get the biological father to go to the lawyer's office to sign the papers. Our lawyer said that we shouldn't have the biological mother sign away her rights until the father did because he could change his mind and keep the baby to himself if the mother signed first. The mother used her leverage to get him to sign. If he didn't, she would keep the baby and ask for child support from him.

It was a nerve-racking time waiting for him to show up. Twice he didn't show up and Michael offered him a ride. When asked why he wasn't following through, he said he wanted to see Nathan before he signed, a reasonable request. We made an appointment, and I took Nathan to meet his biological father. He finally signed and all we needed was the biological mother's signature.

At that time in Arizona, there was a wait time of six months until the adoption went before a judge to make it official. Finally, the time had come, and we were so excited! The judge commented that this was his favorite part of his job. Nathan was finally all ours. We are truly blessed. I was told many times I could not have children before I had my two sons, Skyler and Nathan. Both are gifts from God!

First Hip Revision, 1995

In 1995, during my annual checkup, I was told that my hip was wearing out, and I needed to plan for the first revision of my right hip. A revision is a partial hip replacement because they only replace the ball and socket. I had gone barely seven years without problems; I had been told I should have gone twelve years. I needed to lose weight if I was wanted my hip to stay strong for longer between surgeries.

My physician, Dr. Hugh Thompson III, who I had seen since I was eight years old, finally retired. I was upset because I don't trust many doctors, and I worried about who my new doctor would be. Due to all the problems that I had gone through with being misdiagnosed and neglected, I found it difficult to trust doctors. But I was blessed to have a new doctor take over my case.

In 1995, I had my first revision performed. I couldn't believe how great I felt compared to how painful the original surgery had been. That is something that I have struggled with. I have a disconnect between my head and body. I am not always present in my feelings. I push myself to perform and never give up and when I start to feel better, I push even harder. I only usually end up hurting myself again. Such was what happened two months after my first revision.

I couldn't believe how quickly I was recovering, starting on a walker and moving to a cane after six weeks. It was a miracle to feel so great so soon. But that was short-lived. I was sitting in our rocking chair and watching my boys dance. I was moving my legs up and down to the jazzy music, not thinking of anything, just enjoying the moment. Out came my hip—argh! Just like pop goes the weasel. Yep, I dislocated it. Off to the ER to have it reset.

Unfortunately, it was going to be different this time around. My doctor was on vacation and wasn't due back for a week. I was put into OR to re-set my hip. That went fine but when I woke up, I was in a hospital room and strapped to a foam triangle block to keep my legs and hips immobile. Since my doctor was not available, none of his associates wanted to take responsibility and let me go home. They knew I was young and had a special situation. I got to stay in the hospital for a week until he came home from vacation.

During that time, my parents went to our annual costumers' convention for business owners in Phoenix. I was truly depressed and mad that I had to stay in the hospital. I had looked forward to attending the event with my whole family. My best friend and her family came to Tucson to see me. I was grateful and happy to see them.

When I was discharged from the hospital, the doctor went over my limitations and said to go home and be careful.

Hair, Long Beautiful Hair

In 1974, I'd asked a hairstylist trim my hair, I only wanted like an inch cut off, but she cut off six inches. I swore I would never let anyone else touch my hair! Of course, that was silly and, fortunately, my sister Joyce became an excellent hairstylist. She is the only person I let touch my hair now. I let my hair grow for twenty-five years without a major cut, just trims. It was full, thick, and long, going past my waist to my hips. My hair was a rich, light blonde color. It was beautiful and I loved it! My sister was able to use me as a model for hair shows. She practiced braiding, weaving, and making cornrows. I loved it!

When I married Michael, he loved it too and told me to never cut my hair. I had no problem agreeing to that. I was very protective of my hair, I hated anyone touching it or petting it. I usually wore it up in a bun or in French braids to limit the petting. But as the years passed, I started having headaches from wearing buns, and I didn't want to get a bald spot on my head like my great-grandmother Mattie did. It made me consider getting a real haircut, and I started looking into new styles.

At my sister's salon, there was a woman who could make computer-generated pictures of a client's face with different hairstyles. This was it, I could get Michael to see the pictures and have him pick which one he liked. In my mind, if he picked one, that would be confirmation that he said *okay*. I showed him the pictures and which ones I liked. He said, "If I had to pick one, it would be that one." He had picked a shoulder-length hairstyle. I felt I had the green light to go ahead with the hair appointment. Boy, was I wrong!

I had the appointment with my sister and I felt good about the decision. She cut off fifteen inches. Just like that, it was gone. I went home and my husband looked at me and said he hoped I had a wig on. When I said no, he came over and grabbed the sides of my head and gently pulled. He could not believe I had done it, I had cut off my long, beautiful hair. He was so mad; he hardly spoke to me for a week. In looking back at that whole experience, I realized he never would have agreed for me to cut my hair, so I guess that's why I did it that way.

I think most men love long hair because it is so soft. It doesn't get processed and hair sprayed, which makes hair stiff and hard. I loved the softness, but I couldn't handle the headaches.

As time passed, I continued to get my hair styled. I soon missed the quick hairstyles I was accustomed to. Now, I needed to blow dry my thick hair, use a curling iron, and hairspray the finished look. It took over an hour just to do my hair. Ugh! I started getting my hair cut shorter and shorter. I realized I had a natural curl to my hair, and I didn't have to work so hard to look good. I just had to work with the curls by washing my hair and putting in mousse, and it would stay cute and curly.

When I first thought about cutting my hair, I was worried about no longer having beautiful hair. When it was long, I received compliments from everyone about the length, and the thickness, and the color. I took great pride in my hair. Was I willing to give that up? I decided *yes*, so I did get it cut. But to my great surprise, the compliments continued about my thick, curly hair. Women often say how much they wish their hair was curly so they didn't have to pay for their hair to be curled.

I have no regrets. I loved my short hair; it amazed me how light my head felt compared to having long hair. My cut hair was what they considered "virgin hair," which means it had never been treated, so it was sent to Locks of Love, a company that makes wigs for cancer survivors. I wanted it to be a blessing to someone else who wanted long beautiful hair.

It was just after Nathan was born that I was having difficulty with pain in my right knee. I had been going to the doctor and had several procedures to relieve my pain. I had received shots to help with the pain and physical therapy, but I still couldn't stand on it for very long. All the surgeries and therapy my right leg endured had caused problems, and I was struggling now. My doctor did not want to replace my right knee, he felt I was too young to have it done. Knee replacements are only estimated to last ten to fifteen years, and they are hard to do revisions on, which could cause other problems. He ordered me a knee brace. It was an industrial sports knee brace used by athletes to protect their knees.

I went to get fitted for the brace, which entailed putting a cotton sleeve over my leg and molding it, much like how they would cast a broken foot. I talked myself through most of it, reminding myself not to get upset. This was going to help me walk and be able to do more things. I was pretty strong about the whole ordeal. They said to come back in two weeks and the brace, specially made to fit me, would be ready.

I thought I was doing well until I tried to leave the parking lot and backed into a car. I sat there just crying. I am a safe driver, but this was crazy. The girl who owned the car came over and said, "Don't worry about it, the car is old." I am grateful it wasn't too bad, and she let me go.

I returned in two weeks and had the brace fitted and adjusted for me. I could work and move around easily. Once I adjusted to it, I had more stamina to stand and walk. I wore that knee brace for four years and had to wear it all the time. I was limited when I wasn't using it. I decided my quality of life was not where I wanted it to be, so I requested a knee replacement.

In retrospect, I should have asked the doctor to do the surgery sooner because I had been limited for so long. My quality of life had become terrible because I couldn't do much with my kids or my husband. Plus, my leg was deformed from strapping on the brace tightly so it wouldn't slip down my leg.

My Church

I was born in a Christian, Bible-believing family, and I don't know where I would be without my faith. I was proud to be a member of Catalina American Baptist Church in Tucson from my high school days until 2015. It was great going to church with my family and watching our children grow up together. My oldest, Skyler, attended Sunday school with his cousin Robbie. They were like two peas in a pod, and they bounced off each other with humor and being ornery. There were times they would be separated because some teachers couldn't handle both of them. I always enjoyed them, so many times I would be laughing with them. I loved that my sisters attended the same church, and the cousins became very close.

When I got married in 1982, we had wanted to wait a while before starting our family, which I wrote about earlier. But when I did get pregnant, my sisters started getting pregnant, too. For the next nine years, one of us was pregnant every year. It is easy to remember our children's ages by counting down the years.

When Nathan was eight years old, he asked Jesus to be his Lord and Savior. We had a new pastor at church, and he wanted whoever helped the new believer to their faith to baptize them. I had the privilege of doing this. I felt so proud of Nathan as well as myself.

I served as a moderator for eleven years at Catalina church. There had been many changes in churches in America. Families were not able to volunteer as much as in the past because adults worked longer hours. It was a hard transition for senior members who had been on councils and had been deacons. All decisions were made by committees. The churches were becoming run by pastors and paid staff more and more, work that had previously been done by members.

Our church had just completed a new two-story building with classrooms in the lower level and a multipurpose room upstairs. It was also going through a building project to refurbish the sanctuary. The church was originally built in the 1950s and had needed an upgrade. We were blessed to have an angel benefactor who covered any costs not raised from our members. The whole project would not have been completed without her.

I stayed as moderator for such a long time, mainly due to the separation of the seniors and the younger members. I knew all the seniors because I grew up knowing them. The trust they had in me was the hope that we would transition into a great future for Catalina.

2003

In January 2003, I had knee replacement surgery. After wearing a specially-made knee brace for four years, I was going to get a new knee. The surgery went great, and I was thankful it was over. I had three months of physical therapy and had to push myself to perform all the exercises. I believe the recovery, in many ways, was harder than the previous hip surgeries, not counting my original hip replacement. I struggled daily doing the exercises. If you don't make your joint move as directed by the physical therapist, you will never regain full motion. I wanted to be healthy and strong, so I worked on it. My mom took me three days a week to the sessions until I was released to drive. My mom said the therapist was mean and worked me too hard. Funny how she said the same as when I was young, she was always very protective of me. I just bucked up and did it. I had been limited so long with having to wear the knee brace, I just wanted to be stronger. I accomplished the task at hand and did great.

The summer after having my knee replacement surgery, I was the leader for our church's summer women's camp. After my knee replacement, I've had difficulty hiking the mountains and hills at Tonto Rim Christian Camp in the White Mountains in Arizona. I had attended the camp during my youth without too much difficulty, but after my knee replacement, I wanted to make sure that I could get up and down the hills safely and quickly. I was able to use an electric wheelchair that a church member offered me. It was awesome for that purpose. I went up and down the hills and was able to cover the whole campus.

That fall, we took our boys to Disneyland. Due to my inability to walk long distances, I was able to use one of Disneyland's electric wheelchairs. It was fabulous because they treated people with disabilities with special privileges. I received a map of Disneyland that showed the special doors and pathways we could use to skip waiting in line. That was truly a blessing. I was able to enjoy the park. I also went to MGM Studios in Orlando, Florida. I was able to use their electric wheelchair and have more special privileges. Those two times were some of the only benefits I felt I received from being handicapped.

Closing the Store

The costume shop had become too challenging. There wasn't enough money to become a successful business, according to what the lawyers and consultants said. I spent almost all my time juggling the income to pay the bills. I felt like all of the money went to the landlord and taxes. I wanted to be the owner, I loved the business and every aspect of being in charge, but the income wasn't there.

When we couldn't make the rent on one of the busiest streets, I moved to a street less traveled. Location, location, location. That's key in business. But we had a specialty store, everyone would flock to us to buy our special merchandise: makeup, masks, hats, costumes, everything to make a costume a hit. Yes, Lown's Costumes was the place to be.

My dream didn't last. I should have seen the signs and cut my losses sooner or found a way to stay on our busy street. I did continue in business for another ten years, struggling until it became too difficult, and we retired. Over time, the pop-up stores took a bigger share of the Halloween business. Instead of opening in October, they began opening in September. It became increasingly difficult to hold our own. I tried everything from offering balloon sales, presents in balloons, selling square dance outfits, opening clown schools, and even taking clown schools on the road. Michael bought a long, enclosed trailer to take Halloween supplies to smaller towns. What we thought was a great idea turned out to be fruitless.

In 2007, it became obvious that it was time to close down. We took three months to close, and that was such a great thing. We had more advertisements for us than we could believe. Lown's Costumes closing was big news. It let Tucson residents have a chance to come and say goodbye. People came with pictures of what they had rented. One person had proposed to his wife and wanted the knight costume if we still had it. Liquidating was a huge job. Michael built a storage unit on our property to hold anything that didn't sell so we could continue liquidating after the storefront was closed. It was a huge loss to our family, but I soon found out that life does go on.

I decided to take a year off after closing the store. During that year, Michael and I worked hard to find businesses that would benefit from our liquidation. Michael traveled all over delivering orders to schools and businesses that had purchased. There was no way that we didn't see God's hand in the closing of the business. As hard as it was to close the business, I believe it could not have been done any better way.

I had secured an apartment on the beach in Oceanside, California for the first week after closing the business. Years earlier we all had gone to Oceanside, and I developed a connection with the ocean. It's peaceful to watch and listen to the gentle sound of the waves. It was hard and emotional to close the store; I was happy to have the trip to the beach to look forward to.

One of the biggest things I learned about myself during my time off was that I am a people person. I never would have thought that, it was a big realization. Without my rigid work schedule, I was home with my boys, but it became boring. I was depressed, working on eBay to liquidate the remaining costume items. I was isolated and realized I needed to get out and be useful, find my purpose, and be around people.

I decided to make 2007 a year of many changes. I wanted to experience things that I hadn't had time to while working full-time.

I've heard that if you want to figure out what you would like to do in a new job, you should volunteer. I wanted to work with a Christian women's ministry, so I went to Family Life Radio and met their women's ministry leader, Betty Warner. She was going to start a Northside Women's Aglow monthly meetings, and I joined the steering committee.

Our first steering meeting was at a local Coco's restaurant. I was able to meet new friends who were interested in starting the group. But after receiving the food we ordered, I felt a big impact on my head! The air conditioner ceiling vent fell out of the ceiling and right onto my head. *Ouch!* I ended up with a huge bump on my head and got to spend the rest of the day in the ER getting CT scans and being kept awake. Fortunately, I only received a bad headache that lasted for a week. I think the impression I made on my new friends will last forever. When I see those friends they still joke that I was the woman who had the ceiling fall on her head. What a great impression to leave everyone with.

After meeting with the women's ministry leader, she recommended I speak with the manager at the radio station and ask if they had a special need for a volunteer. I had already volunteered at their twice-yearly phone-a-thons to document financial donations, so I had developed a relationship with some of the workers. But I wanted something more regular. They asked if I could do the morning radio show. I would have to start at five-thirty a.m. I was going to be the phone screener. The morning drive-time hosts, Emily and her husband Tim answered live questions on air and held contests, too. I would answer the phone and screen the caller to make sure the call was appropriate. I did that every Wednesday for a year, I really enjoyed it.

I believed that looking for work would be easy because I was a business owner. I could wear ten different hats to make sure the business was running smoothly and efficiently. Little did I know that hiring managers don't want to hire previous business owners because someone with that kind of experience doesn't want to follow orders.

I applied everywhere but only interviewed at a few. I had interviewed for store manager at Avenue, a clothing store. I went through three interviews but was told they'd chosen someone else. I was disappointed but kept on looking. I interviewed at Dillard's, but I couldn't move into management until I worked as a clerk and worked my way up. I was hired on the spot. Training was scheduled the next morning. But before I could start at Dillard's, I got a call back from Avenue. Fortunately, the job I wanted there was available now, the person they hired originally was relocating to Phoenix. I was so excited!

Avenue was a women's plus-size clothing store, and my job was a challenge from the start. As the store manager, I had to work forty-five hours a week or more. Sometimes I worked up to fifty hours during the week. Standing ninety percent of the time taxed me in the beginning, but I became used to it, although I did have to find supportive shoes. I worked there for almost five years. I started in July 2008 and by the end of the year, the stock market took a dive, and the retail businesses got hit hard. By the end of my time there, I'd worked for three different owners, one that had bought the company out of bankruptcy and two other district managers. Each one had a different way they wanted things to be conducted, so I was always challenged by what I needed to do. It's a good thing I like being challenged because I'm not sure many people could put up with the constant changes.

Downsizing Our Home, 2009

Michael had a difficult time finding work so we borrowed money from our house's equity. We could not keep up the steep payments. We tried to refinance but the bank denied us. We tried a short sale, but the bank turned down two offers. Walking away from our debt was the only choice left. It was a very difficult decision for us. We had so many hopes for our house like putting in a pool to go with the half court for basketball that was there. But we felt we had no choice.

We proceeded to look for a new home. Michael wasn't working and did the majority of the work. We had to downsize our 3000 square foot home. It had four bedrooms and a huge master bedroom with a walk-in closet. There were also extra quarters for my mother-in-law and a 1500 square foot covered patio that we had added.

Skyler was living in my mother-in-law's space that was attached to the side of the house. Now, he also needed to look for a new home. When he tells the story, he says we left him behind when we chose a new place to live. But it was time for him to move out. He had been living there like he was on his own for over six months.

Michael's mission was to look for a three-bedroom house. He located a smaller home not too far from where we were living, and we started downsizing. Michael sold our larger furniture items. The first to go was our bedroom set, all beautiful, white oak furniture that included a bed, two side shelves, a television cabinet with storage for VHS tapes, and a chest of drawers. Oh, how I loved that furniture. He sold the set and bought new, smaller furniture with the money. He also sold the dining room set (our table could seat ten with the added leaves) and the china cabinet. I loved that set, too.

It was time for me to see the house and some of the new furniture that he bought. Boy, was I surprised! I had seen the home empty when we signed the rental agreement, but now I saw it with the furniture he had picked. I was dumbfounded, it looked nothing like I had imagined. He had purchased Tres Amigo's Mexican wood furniture. This whole catastrophe felt like a step backward. I missed our old furniture style. But after a while, the Mexican wood grew on me. Ten years from that day, we would move into a purple house in the desert that would complement the furniture perfectly.

Another Revision, 2010

In 2010, I decided to find out why I hadn't been feeling well. I decided to have a head-to-toe physical exam and found out that I had fibromyalgia, sleep apnea, metabolic syndrome, and my hip needed a revision.

Surgery was set for summer 2010. It had been fifteen years since my last surgery. I hadn't kept up with annual exams for my hip because I wasn't having any problems, so why go? I was working as a retail store manager and summer would be the best time to take the three months off required for healing. The surgery went as planned. The doctor said that the socket was way overdue for replacement, it had accumulated a lot of calcification and was inflamed. That could have contributed to feeling bad. Because I had endured so many surgeries, he made a nineteen-inch long incision down my leg to make it easier to clean everything out. Wow, it was a mega scar! I had been claiming my back was hurting before surgery, so my doctor checked the lengths of my legs, and sure enough, my right leg was shorter. He added almost an inch to my right leg. It was interesting how I felt taller after the surgery. By the end of 2010, I was feeling stronger and healthier. This time around I had physical therapy at my home. That was a new experience, but I think the service is too expensive. I had a lot of sessions in physical therapy, but I don't think I needed it. However, I enjoyed meeting with the therapist since I wasn't going anywhere.

My children have always been a joy to be around, just as entertaining as Michael. Once, Nathan told me about a friend that he called "Smalls."

I said, "Nathan, that isn't a nice nickname for your friend, even if he is small."

Nathan said, "No, Mom, that *is* his last name." I had been thinking they were just making fun of him because he was small, but that was his last name. Ridiculous.

Another time Skyler was on the top bunk in his room and I was on the bottom. He was munching on something and out of the blue asked, "What's the name of my nuts?" Oh, I was so happy that I, a female, was raising a son to ask difficult, personal questions. I'm patting myself on my back for doing such a great job as a mom! I told Skyler, "Why son, those are called testicles." Then Skyler said, a little frustrated, "Mom, not *those* nuts," and showed me the cashew nuts he was eating.

Dislocation, 2012

Fifty years after the accident that ruined my hip, I dislocated my hip in 2012. The day it happened I was feeling great. There have been many times since my hip and knee replacements that I felt physically better than I had in my thirties. This particular day was one of them.

My car battery was dead, so I asked Michael if I could use his car. He said yes and told me to be careful. I had driven his new Chevy Equinox only once before the previous weekend and had no problems. I got into his car and headed to work. I received a call from my assistant manager, she was running late. The store had a rule that we had to use the buddy system when doing anything like opening the store, going to the bank, etc. But I decided not to listen and get the mail by myself. The mailbox was in a kiosk out on the street where our main signage was.

I had done this many times in the four years that I had worked there. I got the mail with no problems, but when I got into Michael's car, I hit my right knee on the steering wheel with so much force and momentum that it pushed the hip joint out of its socket. I had dislocated my hip. Part of the problem was that where I had parked was close to the curb, five to six inches higher than the car. So, I was taller now. I have dealt with an excruciating amount of pain in my life, but this was something new! Tearing the ligaments and muscles was horrible. I was wedged between the steering wheel and the car seat. I was stuck. This was not an easy thing to do. If I had focused on getting in the car, this whole thing could have been avoided.

Thankfully, my cell phone was on my passenger's seat, not in the bag where I usually kept it in the back seat. Before I called for help, I leaned my front seat back and was able to release the pressure on my leg and straighten it out. I called 911 and soon heard sirens. Lots of help arrived!

I asked my co-worker to call my husband and have him meet me at the hospital. My husband has a very bad reaction when events happen outside of his control. He becomes furious. I couldn't deal with that while I was hurting so bad, so I left the task up to her. But Michael had a reason this time to be upset since he was stranded at home with no way to see me. Fortunately, my sons were there to help him through it.

I was praying, angry with myself while waiting for the EMT's to arrive. I never expected anything like this to happen. I had hoped that after my last hip revision I would be able to go another fifteen years until the next surgery or problem. Oh, I was so wrong.

It wasn't long before the EMTs and firemen showed up. What a dilemma I gave them, how would they get me out of the car? The Chevy Equinox was not too big of a car. One of the EMTs tried to give me an IV. I told him that my veins are very hard to draw from. They are deep, like to roll and are tough when I'm not hydrated. Two of them tried to find a viable vein. I showed them the best place to poke me, but it still took three pricks to get the IV going. While this happened, I listened to the firemen talk about how to remove me. I had both my legs straight out, and the back of my chair was leaning back. If I didn't move, I was okay, but when I started moving it was painful.

One option they discussed was removing the top of the car. *No, that's not going to happen, it's a new car.* Another one said to take me out of the back window. I have never been small, there's no way they would have been able to lift me to do that. The next option was to take me out of the opposite side in the back.

I finally said, "I think if you give me enough morphine to take away the major pain, I could lift myself with your assistance and get both feet out the driver-side door."

"Do you think you could do that?" they asked.

"I have very strong upper body strength," I replied. "So, I could use the open sunroof for leverage to lift myself."

Mind you, it was June in Arizona, 110 degrees outside and the car was black. We were all hot and realized we needed to act fast to get me out. First, I needed the medication. It took three shots of morphine until I could move with less pain. The pain never left, but it became bearable. This was another instance where I thanked God that I have a very high pain threshold. Once I was out, we were on the way to the ER.

I was taken to the closest hospital, which was not my regular doctor's hospital. The ER doctors put me under and attempted to reset the hip but had no luck. So they attempted to find an orthopedic doctor that practiced at that hospital and found an associate of my doctor. I was in the ER all day, waiting until he was available. I was admitted to the hospital and prepped for surgery just in case they needed to open the hip. Luckily, with assistance from my doctor's associate, they were able to reset my hip.

When I woke up, I was in my hospital room with my husband and one of my sons. I was grateful for this situation to be over, although it wasn't quite yet.

I was instructed to remember my restrictions and limitations, use a cane, take my time, and know that my muscles would get stronger. They also informed me that the doctor had ordered a hip abductor brace to limit my movement for four to six weeks, and I had to wear it all the time. I thought it was better than wearing another body cast. It was late, so I bid my family goodbye and went to sleep. Or at least attempted to sleep, but waking up every three hours for a checkup makes that difficult. The hospital is a terrible place to get some rest!

I stayed in the hospital overnight and was released the next day. While I was in the hospital, the back of my head kept hurting. Turns out I had thrown my head back and hit the door frame because of the pain. I hope I never have to experience anything like it again. Little did I know, this was the beginning of a three-year journey filled with constant pain and struggles from the damage done to my hip.

I woke up feeling pretty good considering everything I had gone through in the previous twenty-four hours. The nurse told me that the Hanover Prosthetic company was due to see me in a few short hours. I watched TV and waited. There was not much else to do.

After a little bit, a young gentleman came in carrying the brace and a bag. Wow, it was a big brace, much larger than I expected. But I guess I didn't know what to expect.

He started telling me, "You will have to keep this on twenty-four/seven. Do not take it off for four to eight weeks. No showers, you will have to take sponge baths. Going to the bathroom will be difficult, so don't wear any underwear."

"Um, what?"

I repeated all the requirements back to him, and he confirmed the rules. I was alone with him in the room, and he measured me. I started crying uncontrollably. I was having a subconscious moment. My brain was remembering all the times I was in casts and braces, and I didn't want to go through that again. I didn't know what to do. I think this is what some people would call a mental breakdown. Not pleasant at all.

I thank God that I have always had a supportive family and great friends because now was the time I needed them. When I started to cry uncontrollably, the poor guy said he left something in his car and needed to go get it. Off he went. I sat in the hospital room just blubbering. I knew I needed help, I was frantic. I started calling people with the hospital's phone. First, I called my husband. He had his own injury to deal with at the time and wasn't sure when he could make it. I called my oldest son but received no answer, so I left a message. I called my sister and my best friend, but no one answered. I kept leaving messages. My phone was with my bag in the car, and I only knew a few phone numbers by heart. I chose not to call my mom and dad because they were older (seventy-eight and eighty, respectively). They might be upset if I called them. It was hard feeling desperate and lost.

I wondered why I continued to have problems with my hip. I needed help and just started praying. I should have started with prayer, but frankly, I was a mess and wasn't thinking clearly. Support and help were needed—right now! After I called everyone, I sat in the bed, trying to calm down.

In only minutes, my mother called me. She must have known I was going to need her. She said, "I will be right there." Then my husband and younger son showed up. I couldn't believe that my husband had come. Seeing the two of them was awesome. Next, my best friend showed up. My sister called back and said she would be on her way later. Yay! Praise the Lord that I was reprieved with the security of my friends and family nearby, no better feeling than that. I knew I could get through this.

> *I love the Lord because he hears my voice and my prayer for mercy, because he bends down to listen, I will pray as long as I have breath! Psalm 116 1:2*

I had four people with me for support, I was feeling relieved and blessed. They had heard my cry for help, and they had come. The brace fitter even looked a little startled because he had left the room with only me in it and now it was full.

He proceeded to fit me into the huge brace. It looked like an oversized gun holster. It had a wide belt that fit around my waist and attached with strong Velcro straps. It also had a leg wrap that fit around my right leg and a very strong metal piece connecting the two. It limited how much my hip could move and how I could sit down. It was lined with a felt-like material to make it as comfortable as possible. This was going to be my friend for at least the next month. Ha!

I was told not to get out of bed until the physical therapist came to show me what I could do and how to move. I prayed and hoped this would be the last time I needed a brace, but, again, I was wrong.

It's funny how things work out. I was at a place where I believed my hip was great and didn't have any worries about it. Just as the thought crossed my mind, I injured myself.

When I returned to work after three months, I learned a lot about my job. The six-month inventory was on the calendar for the first of October. Once I heard that, I decided not to return until inventory had taken place. A week before I returned, I found out that the acting store manager quit. I began to question things. *Why had she quit?*

I returned to work the day after the inventory. It took about a month to get the results: the inventory showed a loss of 20,000 items. That's $200,000 in income if the items were ten dollars each but of course there were so many items that could have been more than $10. *Oh my* goodness! For the three months I had been out, something evil was happening! I could not believe it. People I'd hired had stolen from the company big time. It was very disappointing.

The loss prevention manager came down to interview all the employees. Everyone was given an appointment time and each employee was interviewed, including me. The acting assistant store manager who was covering for me had taken advantage of the power she had with the store keys. The inspector got her to confess to loading items out of the back door and taking them to sell at the swap meet. She was fired on the spot. The loss prevention manager said they would prosecute her. I couldn't believe it, someone I trusted had done this.

Two months before Christmas, I was without an assistant manager. Now I had to work fifty to sixty hours a week and two days a week I had to open and close the store. I was using a cane and saw no way to keep up the pace. My district manager said since I'd hired the thief, she was going to help me interview and chose the correct person. She ran some ads for available openings.

The interviews came and went. She chose three people, and I called them to make an offer. I started all three at the same time, but guess what? Only one showed up. Yep, my district manager sure knew how to find the right person for the job. I went back to the applications and hired two of the people who I felt would be a great fit, and one of them became one of my best friends.

I worked during that holiday season with no assistance. The hours went on and on. I hurt my left foot, and it ached all the time. Looking back, I find it interesting that I was able to put in those long hours while hurt. I didn't want to quit my job, and I had recently taken three months off. I needed my job—I held the medical insurance that my family needed. Michael, at the time, was responsible for our teenage son. One of us needed to be home when he returned from school each day. I never wanted to be less than other workers, I wanted to be strong and normal, whatever that is.

I stuck it out through Christmas and the start of the new year. Finally, I couldn't stand the pain anymore and saw my podiatrist. The podiatrist said, "So how long have you been walking on your broken foot?" I told him about a month. Most people would have been crying and in considerable pain, not able to walk at all, let alone work! I told him about my high pain threshold, and he said it was an incredible one.

This made me know for sure it was time to find another job. He was in complete agreement. I left his office with an adjustable air-inflated boot that I had to wear for six weeks. When I went back for a checkup after the six weeks, he said I needed another three weeks of healing in the boot. I was still doing too much.

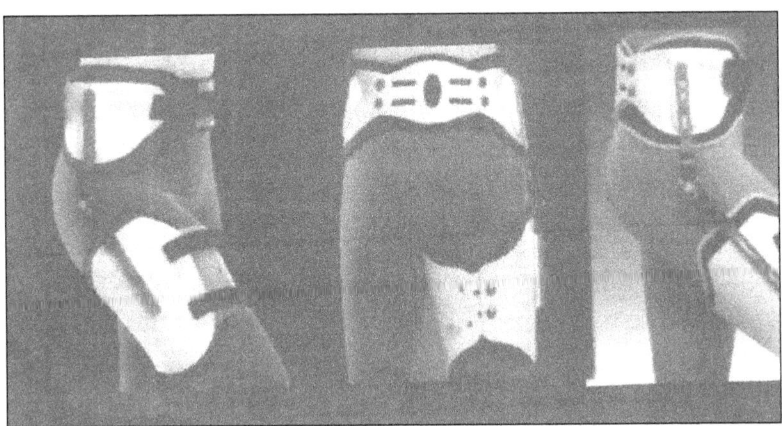

Infection, 2013

I decided to start looking for a new job. I hate the impersonal way we look for a new job. There is no face-to-face interaction until an employer sees your application and calls to set an appointment. Everything is online, too. When I was hiring employees, I used to put up signs and tell everyone I knew that I was hiring. When someone came in to apply, I could interview on the spot if I wanted. It was personal—smile at each other and see each other's eyes. Then, I would know if he or she would be a good fit. That way of hiring was in the past. Ugh!

Job hunting now involves joining all different hiring websites, uploading your application, answering questions, and then waiting to hear back. Definitely depressing. I felt that the places I applied to wanted me to go back to school. At fifty-four, I did not want to go back to school, so that was annoying. Plus, I felt my life experience should be enough. I know we never stop learning, but a structured school setting is not for me. No more! I hated school when I had gone. It's a social nightmare for anyone who doesn't fit in. To me, school was difficult and always discouraging, a brutal experience.

Maybe I just didn't get it. I never hated being myself, I just wanted to be accepted despite all my physical challenges. I guess now that kind of behavior is called bullying. Being bullied because of my physical limitations made me more insecure and scared.

By March of 2013, I was hired as an inside sales associate at a bookstore. I was so excited because it was a sit-down job. The world was changing; the book warehouse was losing sales as the Internet took over. People were using phones or Kindles instead of buying real books. I called to ask accounts where purchases had gone down to see if anything could be done. The majority of the area I was responsible for was the Southwestern states and National Parks. I thought it would be an easy job. I created a book with the list of the business, made records showing their loss in purchases, documented my calls and any information I received.

I spent most of my day on the phone, which was something I did tire of, but I felt I was doing exactly what I was hired for. On one particular Friday, after I'd been there two months, our server for the computer went down. The only working computer was in a closet, and we all took turns using it. It was my turn, and as I twisted into the chair my right hip dislocated. Just like that, it was out. I was panicking, not sure what to do, worried that I couldn't get out of the closet. I sat there for a minute seeing if I really did dislocate my hip, praying for help from God.

I finally called out to a co-worker for help. I'll spare you the details, but I had to be put to sleep and have my hip reset again. I was barely at my new job for two months when this happened. There was only one month left until my three-month probation was over. I was afraid of losing my family's health insurance that I had through my employer.

After being released, no one told me to do anything different, so I returned to work on Monday with a cane. I pushed myself to ignore the pain and work, I didn't want to be fired from my job.

With only a few days to go until my three-month probation was lifted, I was summoned to a meeting with my boss and the outside sales members. I was excited to be included and meet these people who I have been talking to for the past three months. The morning went great and we broke for lunch. Just as I was going to join everyone else in the breakroom, my boss asked me to come to his office. He was a difficult man who had married for money. Not sure what was going on, I thought maybe he would tell me how great I was doing and talk about the last three months. I couldn't have been more wrong. He was letting me go.

"It just didn't work out," he said.

I was so surprised, why was this happening? I thought, "I am a hard worker and did the job he set out for me to do." But I didn't work out, wow! I had never been fired from a job.

Why would he ask me to attend the meeting with other sales associates and then fire me in the middle of it? I asked what I did wrong, but all he'd say was, "It just didn't work out." I believed it all stemmed from me dislocating my hip while I was working. It didn't matter that I went right back to work, ignoring my health. He didn't want the liability since I had health problems.

He told me to take my things and leave. I boxed up my stuff while everyone else was socializing and eating. How insulting. I don't think I have ever felt so embarrassed as I did then. I ended up leaving feeling hurt, angry, and confused.

I was unemployed and wondered what was in my future. I have always liked doing creative projects, so I decided I would repaint my outside furniture. Michael had bought it when we lived in our other house as an anniversary present, and I loved it. It had a base of black paint with turquoise paint sponged over it. We had it for over ten years, and it was rusting, desperately in need of a facelift.

Nathan said he would help me, too. I began painting it, starting with Rust-Oleum paint to help stop the damage from rust. We were close to having the project done. The table and three chairs were finished with only one left to go. But on this particular day, life had a different plan. I started to work on the final chair, leaned forward, and my right hip dislocated. Truly all I did was lean forward, and it felt like my hip wiggled a little, and out it came.

Of course, I was home by myself and my phone was ten feet away. How was I going to get someone to come and help me call 911? I began yelling, which I did for some time. It was 100 degrees, and I was wearing shorts out in the backyard. I finally decided I needed to do something or I would get sunburned. I crawled over to the phone and, after what seemed like an eternity, called 911. The concrete was hot and rough, I felt like I dragged myself rather than crawled. As I waited for an ambulance, my pugs Otis and Peaches came over, wanting to help but licked me instead. There's not much they could do to help anyway.

For those keeping count, this was my fifth hip dislocation. I don't think I ever will get used to it.

When I saw my doctor, he said, "It's time for a revision."

Everything went smoothly after my revision surgery until my incision began oozing fluid. I called the doctor and explained what was happening. His advice was to call back Monday if it continued over the weekend.

Michael kept saying, "Something is wrong, this is not normal." The incision continued to ooze, was a mess to keep clean, and stunk.

When I called my doctor back, he told me to come in immediately, which I did. He told me that I had an E. coli infection that had attached to my artificial hip during my hip revision. My doctor looked sick when he told us. He had no idea how it happened because the hospital has certain protocols to ensure the environment is sanitary and this was a new building only three months old.

The first line of defense was to cleanse my hip, which meant opening the incision and cleansing it with antibiotics. The incision continued to ooze after that surgery, so they did a third surgery and another cleansing. But the incision continued to ooze. It was time to call an infection specialist.

At the Southern Arizona Infection Specialist's office, I started intense antibiotic treatment, which entailed having a peripherally inserted central catheter, or PICC line, inserted into my artery. This allowed the daily infusion of antibiotics to go through my body. The PICC line was essentially an IV line that started in my upper right arm and went into my artery where the medicine could be administered into the jugular vein. The needle and outside tubes needed to be cleaned and replaced weekly. I also picked up antibiotics that had to stay cold and that came in small balloon-like portions, which I administered nightly.

I did this for two months. During that time, the IV in my arm was replaced twice I had to go to be x-rayed so they could make sure it went into the correct location. My infection doctor was amazing. I saw him weekly and he shared my belief that I was going to be healed from this infection. He told me he had never before told anyone who had this infection that they could go off of antibiotics and be healed. With having the bacteria E. coli in the bowels that's always in our system, my infection was the E-Coli being in the wrong place, attached to my artificial hip prosthetic.

During my infusions, I had a visit with my orthopedic doctor who told me a spacer would need to be put in if the infection didn't clear up. This meant I would be on a walker for six months to give the hip joint time to heal and stop the infection. I left his office, sat in a chair in the hall, and just cried. I prayed to God for help because I saw no way out and was devastated.

The next time I saw my infection doctor I shared my fear and without any hesitation he said, "Can I pray with you?"

What? "Of course," I replied. He prayed for a miracle and for my infection to be healed. I found great peace in him praying for me and my belief that I would be healed had been restored. After he prayed, my incision stopped oozing and the healing began.

I completed two months of treatments for the PICC line, and I was prescribed daily antibiotic pills. It would take another two years on antibiotics until I would hear the words I believed I would hear.

"Jacline, I don't get to tell people this very often, but you are healed!" I knew I would hear it, and it came to pass. Another miracle in my life, praise the Lord!

During this time, I was going crazy at home not working. I decided to get rid of some business clothing since I didn't see another full-time manager job in my future. I wanted to bless some plus-size women in need, so I did some research and found a clothing ministry that helped women called Eagles Wings of Grace. I met the executive director and founder, Cynthia Palmer, and asked her if I could volunteer from home. I believe it was God speaking to me, telling me to ask. She said I could update client information for them. I did this for a few weeks and then asked if they received any broken jewelry that I could fix. I love working on jewelry, creating it as well as fixing it.

Cynthia and I grew closer over time to where she would call me out of the blue to check up on me. I was touched by this, she usually called when I was very low and feeling I would never get cured. She prayed with me many times, which always gave me hope that I could persevere. Cynthia asked me when I was feeling better if I would consider joining the Eagles' board of directors. I was honored to be asked. I had no idea that in the coming years I would become the president/executive director of Eagles Wings of Grace.

My best friend Susie was another godsend during this time. She would come over to just spend time with me, bring me things, and be a good friend. I had hired her back in 2011 to work at Avenue, and we became close. In September 2014, we received a call that Susie had passed in her sleep. She had sleep apnea, which both Michael and I suffer from. We had told her many times to look into it because she had fallen asleep at the wheel while driving to school and hit a trash can. She was a kindergarten teacher, a great one. She loved kids and being a teacher.

We gave her a sleep apnea machine and encouraged her to be tested. She was able to get tested and get the machine set to the pressure level she needed. The sad thing is, she wasn't using it. It was right next to her on the bedside table. I feel a great sense of loss and miss her to this day.

Please if you snore, and you're not getting the needed amount of sleep, take care of yourself and get tested.

Turning Sixty, 2017

The year I turned sixty started great. I was volunteering at Eagles Wings of Grace as a board member, and my health was improving. But by the end of the year, I would be asked to take on all the responsibilities of the ministry because the president and founder was retiring to Michigan. It was a shock because I didn't think that that would happen so quickly. Similar to when I was handed my parent's business. I had felt it may happen someday but didn't know when.

Recently, I had fallen in the shower and had cut my shin above my right ankle. Any fall is not good, but this one was bad because I developed a hematoma under the small cut that wouldn't heal. I was sent to the wound care section of the hospital and had to go weekly for eight months. I could not believe my poor luck. I had to wear a wound vacuum for the first four months. It seemed like it was never going to end. I was finally released from wound care after eight long months.

But before my release, Michael planned the biggest birthday party ever for me. That year, my birthday was on a Saturday, and Michael invited everyone we knew. He took a picture of me as a two-year-old and made it into an enormous poster that he put out front to indicate which house was ours. Partygoers saw the picture before heading to the backyard for the celebration. Michael made three extra-large pans of sour cream enchiladas for the entree, wine coolers and Coke for the drinks, chips and dip for the snacks, and, of course, a huge birthday sheet cake for dessert.

It was the best birthday party I've ever had. I wore a tiara because it was my party and, hey, I was now sixty years old. By the end of the night, all the food and drinks were gone. We had sixty-two attendees. It was amazing! The neighbors said there were cars everywhere down the street and around the corner. I doubt that I'll ever have a better birthday.

Saying Goodbye to My Parents, 2018

We had gotten my mom into respite at the Fountains Assisted Living in the fall of 2013 because she was failing. We could no more take care of her needs so she agreed to go to live at the Fountains in Tucson. With investigating the financial support that they could receive from the Military, we found out both my mom and dad had to live together as the same facility. It was hoped after three months that mom's health would improve from being so frail so she could move to independent living and my dad would join her.

The Fountains also had Independent Living facility and they had an apartment on the first-floor available. It was a one-bedroom apartment with a patio and area for their dog. It was perfect, we got ready to move them in and planned where all the furniture would go. They were so excited.

Just a couple of days before the move, we received a call from the office asking if my dad had been reviewed and was approved for the move. I replied that I wasn't aware that he had, but didn't feel it was a problem. Unfortunately, we were wrong. He didn't pass the incontinence and dementia tests.

My dad wanted to stay in his home if he couldn't be independent, but my mom wanted to stay in the assisted living part of The Fountains. She wanted them doing her laundry and cooking her meals, the things that were hard for her to do. But due to their tight finances, my mom couldn't stay without my dad. So they decided to move dad into assisted living, they didn't have any openings for a bigger room but they would have rooms next to each other, sharing an outside patio. They could keep their car and their little dog, Sandy, but they had to let go of so much stuff in their home where they'd lived for forty-six years.

Frustrated, my mother blamed my father for not being able to move into the independent living tower. The next five years spawned many arguments with my mom over not wanting her husband to come into her room. She became an angry, unhappy person. I spent a lot of time talking her down, trying to get her to draw on her Christian faith and see what her purpose was. I wasn't successful in this endeavor. She never liked the homes she moved into whether she'd chosen it or my sister and I chose it. She left three because she moved into a geriatric mental health care facility. We moved my mom five times in five years, which was very expensive and a whole lot of work.

In August 2018, my dad started trying to leave The Fountains to be with my mom. He never held anything against my mom except confusion about the treatment he received from her. He loved her and wanted them to be reunited. His health couldn't allow him to live independently. His final accident happened when he fell down two flights of stairs with his walker and lost a shoe. The office nurse said his dementia had advanced and he needed more care than they could provide. The home wasn't equipped to watch him at all times. Someone would have to stay with him twenty-four/seven until we were able to find him a new home.

It only took a few days and we moved him to a memory care home where he shared a room but could have his own TV and personal items. Granted, he had much less than what he had in his last assisted home.

My dad's dementia began to get worse. He hated his new home and missed his friends and the food. He wanted to go back, but of course, he couldn't. Two months later, we could see he didn't have much life left to live. He could no longer stand and needed help getting up and down. He was moved into hospice.

My sister, Joyce had heard of a military program where a member of the military would come and honor him for his service with a lap blanket and a plaque. We invited all the family members. Joyce had made a picture display of his military tours and metals. My mother chose not to come, which was a great disappointment for all.

It seemed as though this was the beginning of the end. As his health declined, the hospice called and said he might pass within a couple of days. We began preparing for the end. Everyone knew he was having quite painful moments. We kept the hospice nurse busy with requests to make him comfortable. It was awful. It was the longest week of my life. Hospice kept saying, "It should be today, it should be today."

His strong body was slowly dying. My mom came to stay with him for a few days. We spent the time reminiscing, praying, and talking to him. My mom said something interesting—she said that I didn't know everything about my life story, that she and dad had not told me everything.

"Curious," I thought. "As now I'm sixty-one, and I surely should be able to handle everything." It made me upset, not that I wasn't upset enough about my dad dying, but this bit of information was ridiculous.

Then, she said to dad, "Do you remember when we saw Jackie on the plane after she was missing for four days?" I thought I was missing for three days, and now she's saying it's four? Her comment added to my confusion, but I don't want to be remembered by that horrible incident. Lots of memories are happier than that.

After my mom brought up the past, I felt compelled to talk to my dad. I spent time talking to him while it was just he and I. I apologized for the accident that changed the family dynamics and what I believe had stripped my mom of her peacefulness and happiness. I apologized that he had to deal with her challenges and emotional issues. If I could have changed anything about my life, I would have never crossed the street without using the crosswalk. I think I've finally stopped blaming myself for the accident. I should never have been with my five-year-old sibling brother crossing a street without an adult. We were too young to go alone to bring my other brother home. We all paid the price for my horrible accident, which I know that everyone also wished had never happened.

Some of the caretakers from the Fountains heard my dad was dying and came to say goodbye. Dad was such a loving, kind person that everyone who knew him loved him back. It touched me that they would take the time to honor him.

On the seventh day, Joyce and I had been there with him as much as we could be and left him late at night. It wasn't long until he was gone, and his hospice called to let us know he was at peace. Praise the Lord, we know where he was, and he is truly at peace.

After my dad's passing, I asked my mom about what she said. Her reply was that she couldn't handle telling me that right now. "Why would she bring the past up during such a difficult time?" I wondered. It always seemed that she would say things just to upset me, like making me suffer for causing the accident. Truly not fair.

Dad's memorial service was a celebration of his life.

The eulogy stated, "*He leaves behind fifteen grandchildren, one of whom preceded him in death, and six great-grandchildren. John was loved by anyone he met. He was a God-loving man who was active in his church for over forty years, holding many positions. And now we say goodbye to Old Shaver.*"

My dad referred to his grandsons as Little Shaver, especially my son Skyler. So, he became Old Shaver. It was an endearing way to communicate with his grandsons. He truly is missed by all.

A New Knee

As I write this, I am waiting for yet another surgery. After sixty-two years of my stronger leg taking the brunt of my weight (more than any leg should take), my left knee is done. I did gel injections, exercised, and took ibuprofen each day to try and postpone this surgery. I even got a marijuana card but didn't like how it made me feel. The only plus was I was able to sleep through the night.

I fell three times in two weeks and strained my right knee, the artificial one. I was alone when I fell the third time. I landed right on my kneecap and was fearful that I'd broken my kneecap or damaged the artificial parts. I couldn't put any weight on my right leg. I now believe I fell because with my left knee was hurting. I wasn't picking up my left foot high enough to clear rugs, curbs, or anything in my way and down I went.

At the urgent care at Northwest Hospital, the X-rays were inconclusive, so they did an MRI on my right knee. The doctor's first diagnosis was that I had a hairline fracture on my femur bone. All I could do was cry, not realizing what that would mean for recovery, but I knew it sounded bad. I looked up and saw my youngest son, Nathan. He came to give me support and was a breath of fresh air. I needed that more than I could say.

When I'd decided to take myself to urgent care, I chose to not call anyone until I knew what the prognosis was. Once I found out, I called Michael. He was away in Phoenix for work and Skyler was out partying. (It was his goodbye party. He was moving to Portland for a new opportunity the following day.) Next, Nathan was called, and he was my savior that day.

I immediately asked the doctor if I could be transferred to Tucson Orthopedic Institute to my orthopedic specialist, about a forty-five-minute drive across town. The whole journey across town I settled down a bit, no longer crying but praying like crazy for a miracle.

At the hospital, they put me on the fourth floor where they do surgeries. It became clear that they had plans for me to go to surgery. No food, no water, no nothing. Yikes. The reality that I may need another surgery was settling in.

But then, the orthopedic doctor on call said that there was no fracture. Praise the Lord, it was a *miracle*! An X-ray technician and two additional doctors confirmed the results. It was truly a miracle. I felt blessed!

The doctor said they would order a knee brace, and I could probably go home tomorrow. But I would have a knee brace and be on a walker for who knows how long.

I wore the knee brace for six weeks and was on the walker for three months. I was scheduled for a new knee, too. I am sure that the knee replacement surgery was my most painful surgery, even though I don't remember the surgeries I had when I was little. Well, it's actually physical therapy that is the painful part—they make you work. The first knee replacement I had was in 2003, I had worn a knee brace for three years prior, which had made the muscles very weak. This meant my physical therapy was more intensive and brutal.

I'm glad to say that my second replacement is behind me. And yes, it was as bad as the first, only now I was sixteen years older. With all my hip surgeries being painful nothing compares to a knee replacement, I can truly say I am glad I only have two knees, the physical therapy is what makes it so tough.

Recovery

Food = Drug of Choice

Addiction is a sign that a person is divided from their truth. You have uncomfortable feelings, and food lets you stay numb and block the feelings out. I was never shown at an early age how to deal with my sadness, pain, grief, or anger in a healthy way. Binge eating became a stuffing down of difficult emotions. Instead of processing my feelings, I would eat.

But that's not how it has to be, I can change the pattern that is deeply ingrained in me. I can step back and observe it and consciously replace it with a new pattern. When I decide to eat, I need to stop and observe what triggered the desire to eat. As a bystander, I observe and can choose to stop eating or go ahead and eat. Being present and aware makes a difference. With this awareness, I have lost sixty pounds. I still have about forty pounds to go, but I am on my way to be a healthier Jackie.

The End

As my story here comes to an end, my journey outside these pages continues. I was fortunate to be born into a Christian family where all the children came to know Jesus at an early age.

My story wasn't put down on paper to solicit any sort of pity. I've spent my whole life trying to be normal. I've always done the very best I could do not to be a victim. I wanted to document a journey that involved all sorts of obstacles and miracles. If I didn't believe that God had a plan for my life, I am sure I wouldn't have been able to survive the constant challenges.

> *For I know the plans I have for you, declares the Lord, plans to prosper you, not to harm you, plans to give you hope and a future. Jeremiah 29:11*

There is so much more to being a Christian than just accepting Jesus as your Savior. It is life *changing*. If you have never made the choice to become a Christian, you can do it right now. Follow the simple ABC acronym:

A – Ask Jesus to come into your heart
B – Believe in Jesus Christ
C – Choose to follow Jesus's teachings

I believe it is so important to accept Jesus Christ as your Savior and develop a personal relationship with Him, walking and talking with Him daily. Start each and every day by thanking God that you are alive and choose to be the best person you can be. End each day by thanking God for His help in getting through another day.

When you need to make decisions or choices it helps if you use the acronym, WWJD, which means "What Would Jesus Do?" When you need to make a decision, pass it through the filter of WWJD to make your decision.

I have also learned over the years that I should use my gut to make decisions. If I feel peace in my decision, I move forward with it. If I don't have peace, then I am making the wrong decision for me. I know that Jesus has been right by my side through each thing that I have been through. That I know without a doubt is my truth.

For the last five years, I have been involved in Eagles Wings of Grace, a Christian clothing ministry and have been the executive director for the last three. When the founder retired in 2017, it was a part-time ministry. It has since grown to a full-time ministry that's helped 328 clients a year in 2017 to 1200 women in 2019. In 2019, we added education classes to teach women basic cooking skills and budget skills. For eleven years, the ministry was managed entirely by volunteers. In 2018, we hired a part-timer and the continuity we needed was provided. In 2020, we moved to a new address on a church property. As we continue to grow the ministry, we change the lives of more and more disadvantaged women. Providing women with business clothing empowers them as they interview for jobs. Learning basic skills like cooking and budgeting is another tool for empowerment. Our work helps them to become a viable asset in their community.

I love what I do. It is wonderful to make a difference in women's lives and work with the most amazing women who donate their time to keep the ministry moving forward. I have great support from my husband. He has said that it was like my whole life had been preparing me for this job.

My life has been amazing. I have been blessed with a wonderful husband who has been right by my side though all my different issues during our forty years together. I have two amazing sons, and I couldn't be prouder of who they have become. I can only imagine how the rest of my life will go. I am retired, but I would prefer to be "re-fired" and make a difference in our lives.

CPSIA information can be obtained
at www.ICGtesting.com
Printed in the USA
FSHW021001120721
83043FS

9 781662 819230